MILLION BILLION

ALSO BY MICHAEL PERRY

BOOKS

Population 485: Meeting Your Neighbors One Siren at a Time

The Jesus Cow

The Scavengers

Visiting Tom: A Man, a Highway, and the Road to Roughneck Grace

Coop: A Year of Poultry, Pigs, and Parenting

Truck: A Love Story

Off Main Street: Barnstormers, Prophets & Gatemouth's Gator

Roughneck Grace: Farmer Yoga, Creeping Codgerism, Apple Golf, and other Brief Essays from On and Off the Back Forty

From the Top: Brief Transmissions from Tent Show Radio

Danger, Man Working: Writing from the Heart, the Gut, and the Poison Ivy Patch

Big Boy's Big Rig: The Leftovers

AUDIO

Never Stand Behind A Sneezing Cow • *I Got It from the Cows*

The Clodhopper Monologues

MUSIC

Headwinded • *Tiny Pilot* • *Bootlegged at the Big Top*

Long Road to You

For more information visit SneezingCow.com.

MILLION BILLION

Brief Essays on Snow Days, Spitwads, Bad Sandwiches, Dad Socks, Hairballs, Headbanging Bird Love, and Hope.

MICHAEL PERRY

The essays in *Million Billion* originally appeared as "Roughneck Grace"
columns in the *Wisconsin State Journal* and are reprinted here with
permission. Many were also featured as monologues on *Tent Show Radio*
(TentShowRadio.org).

CONTENTS

ACKNOWLEDGMENTS

The readers.
So often your kind words are just the nudge
I need to keep at it.

Without Beth Williams, John Smalley, Gayle Worland, Alissa
Freeberg, and Ben Shaw, I'd be typing into the wind.

And always, my family.

INTRO

The first "Roughneck Grace" column was published in the *Wisconsin State Journal* on Sunday, March 3, 2013. I've been writing one a week (give or take a week per year) ever since. Someone asked me once if it was hard to keep coming up with good ideas. "Yeah," I said. "I mean, have you *read 'em* lately?"

I've always tried to be a writer with a small "w," which is to say I work at it never assuming the world is clamoring for my wisdom. Writing a weekly column is a good antidote to creeping pretensions of that sort. You constantly have to ask yourself if you're saying anything new, if you're repeating yourself, or if this week maybe instead of your musings on the meaning of life folks would rather hear how neighbor Denny caught the litterbugs.

The schedule also doesn't allow for a lot of lingering revision. You just gotta get it done and get it in. That's been good for me too. It's like writing as calisthenics as opposed to artful indulgence.

You keep at it, pretty soon you got a stack. The columns in this collection pick up where the book *Roughneck Grace* left off (and *From The Top* before that). In previous collections, the editors and I arranged the pieces by theme; in this book, we've chosen to just let them flow in the order readers received them. For you archivists, the first column in this book published on March 27, 2016; the last on March 25, 2018.

AUNT MABEL

The funerals having lately come one after the other, I had sworn an obituary moratorium, but when Great Aunt Mabel died last week, I knew I'd have to note it.

I can't do justice to her 90 years other than to say, boy, she didn't waste any of 'em. Born up north there in the township of Madge, near Sarona, she commuted to a one-room school-house on wooden skis made by her father. When her school-teacher ordered instruments from the Sears & Roebuck catalog, Mabel and her three brothers formed a family band, and a love of music would be central to her life until the end —in fact, she met her husband Robert at a square dance in the Sarona town hall, and they danced until farmer's lung took him from the dance floor in the 1970's and for good in 1982.

As a teenager she spent summers thinning rutabagas and picking potato bugs in the same fields as German prisoners of war. She also helped on the home farm, where her chores included egg collection, a task she dreaded for all the pecking she endured. By way of revenge, for the rest of her life, every time she ate at a restaurant she ordered chicken.

My memories of Aunt Mabel are divided between my childhood, when she would fry up the fish we brought her, and the last decade or so, when she began showing up at my public performances with a septuagenarian/octogenarian posse, a scene I had in mind when I described her in *Truck: A Love Story*:

Aunt Mabel, eighty years old and currently charging off to every cultural event within a fifty-mile radius of Spooner, Wisconsin, usually with a carload of restless contemporaries.

They were something to see, this perm'd squad rolling up in a minivan with Mabel at the wheel, ready to encourage me during and razz me after. It was lovely to be made to feel like a kid at the school recital again in the very best way.

Right through her final decade she really was up for anything. When my brother asked if she wanted a ride in his two-seater airplane he hadn't even finished the question before she was headed for the cockpit, walking cast notwithstanding. Same when my brother-in-law offered her a ride on his ATV. Same when someone offered her a ride on a snowmobile.

I share this so that when I tell you one of her dearest hobbies was sewing hot pads, you don't think she was just quietly whiling her time away. It started with a few made as tokens of thanks for helpful friends. Then she began donating them for fundraisers, Christmas food baskets, and assisted living facilities. The week before she died, she finished hand-sewing the border on her 8,000[th] pad.

There was a stack of the final batch at the back of the church, and after the service we were invited to help ourselves. Over time Mabel's reputation grew so that people brought her all kinds of fabric prints, from calico to comic. I chose a pair decorated with fire helmets for my firefighter pal Mills, John Deere logos for my collector neighbor Tom, and, for my daughters, based on their favorites, one with cats and one with cowboy boots.

This is just the thinnest gloss on a long, layered life. And a gloss over the stretches that weren't so blithe. But given this space, it will have to do. Words are not the true memorial, nor the headstone, but rather the casserole cooling on the quilted fabric, Aunt Mabel's stitches neat and holding fast.

A SMASHING SOUVENIR

Once when I was old enough to drive but still in high school I took the family van to Bloomer and met my pal Greg at the bowling alley to play racquetball. At one point I tried to hit the ball off the front wall right at the same time Greg tried to hit the ball off the back wall and our racquets crashed together, slicing the pad of my right index finger and smashing the fingernail. By that evening the fingernail was purple, and that night it throbbed so Mom had to do the thing where she heated up a sewing needle on the stove until it glowed then lanced the nail. Medieval, but the relief was immediate.

Getting hurt around Greg was second nature, as the first time we ever met he and his siblings threw rocks at me, although I can't say with certainty he threw the one that hit me in the head. Later, in high school, for sport, he often chased me down the high school hallway while cackling and waving a wooden leg he had ripped from the math teacher's chair. He also once set me loose on a wild horse with a loose saddle cinch just to see if I would survive.

I was always—understandably, I think—a little twitchy

around him, but he was also one of those true-blue rough-neck pals who always had my back. One Friday night we tooled up to Rice Lake hoping to meet girls at the McDonalds. I can't recall the make of Greg's car, but it was big and green and had genuine bull horns mounted above the grille and a genuine cow tail slammed in the trunk so it draped over the back bumper. On our way out of the parking lot after our Big Macs, Greg punched it and sprayed gravel all over some Rice Lake football player's shiny four-wheel drive pickup. The restaurant—which was filled with the rest of the team, as the game had just ended—emptied in a swarm, and we shortly found ourselves in a bona fide car chase. "There's a club in the back seat!" hollered Greg, "Grab it!"

Out of loyalty to our friendship and my own misguided testosterone, I grabbed the club, but in doing so saw four or five well-populated vehicles swerving all around us. At that point I did some math, then informed Greg the answer kept coming up *retreat*. I suppose it was just the kind of lily-livered suggestion he expected from me, but after a quick glance in the mirror he flattened the accelerator and when we hit the city limits the only thing still behind us was that cow tail, flying straight in the wind.

We did have our more tender moments. In 1983, Greg and I were each other's date for prom, a move that could be seen as wildly progressive but may in fact have been the result of limited prospects due to driving around in a big green car adorned with a genuine dead cow tail.

Eventually he graduated, joined the Army, got married, spent time in the desert fixing tanks, came home, and last time I saw him he was a diesel mechanic and had raised a fine son. That's shorthand, but life is quick. If you ask, I'll show you my fingernail, still deformed after all these years. Sometimes waiting at the dentist's office, or on a trip far from home, I look at it and feel my youth as yesterday.

DENNY DINGS DEAD END LITTERBUGS

One of the things you discover when living at the terminus of a dead end country road is a certain segment of the population is possessed of an odd dyslexic-type disorder in which they interpret a yellow diamond DEAD END sign as a DUMP HERE sign. Several times a year we are greeted by all manner of trash and unwanteds tipped out by the mailbox or slung into the wooded verge.

My neighbor Denny lives right at the base of the hill where our dead end road commences, and since he retired he has made it his part-time hobby to keep an eye out for these landfill flouts. A while back he saw an unfamiliar van head up our hill and decided to investigate. He zipped up there on his four-wheeler and caught a pair of knuckleheads making their escape after chucking a bunch of electronics into the ditch. Denny blocked the road and made them load it all back up while he sat there watching them, astride his four-wheeler like some Old West sheriff.

Given this history, when I motored out our tree-lined drive last night only to encounter an upended recliner and sofa sectional on the shoulder it wasn't a complete surprise.

In fact, our sofa is pretty much shot so I slowed down for a quick look on the off-chance it might match our non-existent drapes. Unfortunately whoever did the dumping apparently did so at speed, and while the cushions looked good, the understructure had not survived.

Leaving this windfall behind, I drove to the bottom of the hill and hung a right. Spotting Denny in his yard, I pulled into his driveway and lowered my passenger side window. "Hey!" I yelled. Denny looked up from what he was doing. "You missin' yer couch?"

Denny came over and leaned through the window. I told him about the fractured furniture. He shook his head. "What kinda person thinks that's OK?" I said, and Denny shook his head again, and said he'd found a refrigerator and a toilet in the ditch recently. But then in defense of the common man Denny started reciting how much they charge you when you take a load of junk to the dump these days, and what a rigma-role it is to dispose of appliances, and in fact there are plenty of folks who just don't have that in their budget, let alone their wallet.

That led us to discuss burn barrel fees and how they led to a proliferation of "fire pits" and then we veered off into how it came to be that his ditch out in front of the house there was all ash-blackened and it turns out that story is a real knee-slapper that Denny admits began when he uttered the words "I wonder if this stuff'll burn?" (the pyromaniac equivalent of , "Here, hold my beer!") and shortly led to him running a one-man bucket brigade back and forth between the ditch and his wife's koi pond, and how when she asked him what he was doing he basically said *no time to talk!*

Then we got on to what mighta killed his three roosters and pretty soon we'd shot a good 20-30 minutes through the car window and when I finally pulled out of the driveway headed for where I was headed in the first place I thought,

Well, I wish people wouldn't be grotesque litterbugs, and whoever dumped that living room set I wish I'd'a caught'em when I had my snowplow and some stubble on, I coulda maybe put a little fear in'em, but then again they wound up giving me a reason to stop in and shoot the breeze with Denny, and I'll remember that ditch fire story a lot longer than I'll remember that sofa.

THE FIRST WARM AIR

My younger daughter came skipping up the driveway through the sunlight after school on the first fifty-degree day and announced she wanted to "do something outside tonight." First there were chores—unload the backpack, empty the lunch bucket, collect the chicken eggs, unload the dishwasher, do the math homework. These things accomplished, we met in the yard.

Even in these shifty climate times, even after a winter that could never really get it together and make something stick, the freedom of running outside without layering up or at the very least drawing on boots and a cap is enough to put a bounce in even a flat-footed 51-year old dad's step. We hit the bare yard at a trot.

First we went for the Frisbee. She had never successfully thrown one before, so when she sent it rolling across the yard like some drunken dinner plate on the lam, I showed her how to hold it and flick it with a little spin and shortly she was exclaiming with delight as it crossed the yard on a wobbly float, no small feat considering there was a stiff wind blowing.

Next we used an old golf club to hit avocado pits. After a winter of dumping the pits out with the rest of the food scraps the chicken run is lousy with them. They're a little light and tend to split in two, but they're fun to whack. Not as fun as whacking wormy apples, which we do every fall, but fun enough, and it's entertaining to watch the cats chase the halves. For a finale, I teed up a spoiled clementine, which exploded juicily, delighting the gallery of one.

By now the brisk wind had overcome spring and optimism, so I ducked into the house for a cap and jacket before continuing with Wiffle ball. I did the pitching, she did the hitting, and the cats occasionally fielded. After a few innings and a final inside-the-park home run that may or may not have been aided by my intentional incompetence, I was ready to head in for supper but the tot wanted to play tag. I've got one leg that doesn't quite work right but we were still able to have a fine galumphing time, and she took great delight in hiding out behind the old chicken coop and then dashing off beneath the low-hanging apple tree branches in an attempt to peel me off.

By the time we went into the house for supper I was voraciously hungry in the way I used to get as a youngster tearing around the yard of my childhood. As we sat down to eat with the rest of the family the younger daughter reminded us that since it had just been her ninth birthday she wanted us to measure her after supper and make a mark in the doorway where all the other marks were. She was born in our house and her time of arrival is still faintly visible on the old feed mill chalkboard that hangs on the wall by the chimney. It seems only an ephemeral moment or so ago that I could cradle her entire body in the crook of my arm. Yes, I said, we'll measure you and make a mark, smiling even as I secretly hoped the pressure of the ruler atop her head would somehow slow the seasons.

PRINCE AND THE PURPLE THREAD

Just over two weeks ago, I was working on a book manuscript, and I wrote this:

"Perhaps you failed to guess, but I owe the bulk of my aesthetic construct to Prince Rogers Nelson, circa the movie *Purple Rain*, circa cassette. The film and album were released the summer after I graduated from high school. Come fall, when college was back in session, I had sat solo in the theater watching *Purple Rain* a minimum of four times, worn the hubs off the soundtrack, stocked my bedroom at Grandma's house with purple scarves and fat candles, and scotch-taped fishnet to the drywall above the bed (intended to create shadows of mystery but in reality a most pointless snare). I furthermore spent time snipping words and letters out of old magazines and taping them around the edges of the bureau mirror to re-create Prince's lyrics in the style of a hostage note, phonetic shorthand included (Prince was text message before text message). That very same summer I left Wisconsin to work as a cowboy in Wyoming, made my first trip to Europe, and began experimenting with hair mousse.

"All us cosmopolitans gotta start somewhere."

Of course I wrote this having no idea that Prince would be dead within the week. When I heard the news, I posted the excerpt on my blog. It's tricky, commenting publicly about the deaths of famous people. I'm walking a fine line of leveraging someone's very real personal tragedy to draw attention to myself. I'm throwing encomiums at someone I didn't really know. I'm one of millions saying the same thing, or variations on the same thing. None of it one bit of help to the dead man.

Then again, I also wrote this:

I'm a stocky flat-footed farm boy from Chippewa County, Wisconsin, who can't dance a lick. But Prince in his own purple way set me free. The book I'm working on is about the French philosopher and essayist Montaigne, who once wrote, "I now, and I anon, are two several persons; but whether better, I cannot determine." I think of my young self trying to be Prince, a foolish pursuit on the face of it, but essential at the heart of it, leading as it did to other gracious worlds.

The social media comments that followed my post were heartening. So many people from so many walks of life testifying to how some song, some show, some snippet of film or video, held meaning for them in ways we might never suspect.

One commenter was more concise, writing: "Get a life. Really."

Well sure. There are far grimmer troubles afoot. The fact remains: A very real person did very real work, and it had a very real effect on my life. That doesn't mean I *worshipped* Prince, or thought there was a *perfect* Prince, or that I liked everything he did. Or that my opinions in this instance matter one whit. I'm simply grateful for what he put out there that eased and brightened my clodhopper path.

Get a life?

Did.

Have.

And woven through the blue jeans and flannel and lumpy t-shirts you'll find the thinnest thread of purple.

NOTE: *This column went on to become part of the "Amateur Aesthetics" chapter in the book* Montaigne in Barn Boots.

SWING SET SMUGGLER

My gut seized up a little when the man looked at the 8-foot bed of my old pickup truck and said, "You do realize the top bar of this swing set is 20 feet long, right?"

I did not.

This day was traceable back to my father, a hardworking farmer with an affinity for swing sets. At family reunions in the park, he'd take his turn with the kids, the taller the swing the better. Eventually my brother John built a towering swing set in the yard at Dad's farm, welding the whole works up by himself, fashioning the hangers, the seats, the trapeze. That set has led to thousands of happy hours for adults and children alike, especially when we all gather on Sunday afternoons. My daughters so loved the big swing that they've often asked for one of their own.

Time slips away, so when they asked again last month, I went online and did my research before the swing went the way of the tree house I still haven't built. Got a little sticker shock at what an old-school, playground-style swing costs new. Considered ordering the parts and whatnot, get my own pipes, build it myself. Recalled the unbuilt tree house. Hit up

Craigslist. Not only found an old-school playground-style swing—heavy-duty galvanized pipes, hefty chains, and belt seats—but one from an actual school playground, and at a quarter of the price. Disassembled and ready to go, said the guy on the phone. Only catch was, the set was in a large-ish Minnesota city nearly two hours away. Before I left, my wife asked if I'd verified that the parts would fit in the pickup. Not a problem, I said, meaning I'd "eyeballed" the picture on the Internet. "Okay," she said, in the way she often does when she sees me hurtling toward walls of my own building.

So I stood there in the cold rain two hours from home and realized there'd be more pipe sticking out of the back of the truck than in the truck, and those were the *short* pieces. That twenty-footer was bound to protrude like a wrecker boom.

By the time I left the premises, I'd deployed every available bungee, ratchet strap, and rope in an attempt to secure the pipes. The seller gave me four concrete blocks to weigh down the butt ends to keep them from levering over the tailgate. Finally, digging around in my EMT kit, I found some bandaging tape and used half a roll to affix a blaze orange safety vest to the end of the 20-footer. When I stepped back for a look, the truck was squatting and looked like a homemade anti-aircraft rig flying the flag of some redneck militia.

I didn't even make it through the first traffic circle before the whole works shifted, nearly wiping out a street sign. I had to reposition and re-do all the strapping as the cold rain gullywashed my neck.

The trip home took nearly three hours. I drove every foot of it tensed in anticipation of the rotating red-and-blues in my mirror. One of the neighbors saw me in the final mile. "What the fuzz were you *thinking*!?!?" he said later, or something like that.

Well, I said. My dad liked swing sets. Bigger the better. And now we've got one.

HEADBANGING BIRD LOVE

Woodpecker love is no weirder than any other love, although even at my most twitterpated I was never driven to slam my snoot into solid steel at triphammer speed, as does the feathered fellow who has chosen to broadcast his affection from the tin roof of our woodshed, located very near our bedroom window, especially at sunup.

My ornithology knowledge pretty much tails off after chicken, robin, and blue jay, but thanks to bird books I'm pretty sure our backyard beatmaster is a downy woodpecker. This morning when I investigated I caught a flash of red at the back of its head before it flew, so it's a male, although I'm told females engage in "drumming" also.

"Drumming." Such a lovely, artful, *birdy* term. Brings to mind the airy *whump-whump-whump* of the distant partridge, or the mysterious air-throb of a power-diving snipe; but when this woodpecker decides to broadcast, it's like Rosie the Riveter and Samuel Morse got all jacked on meth and went tap-dancing at the sheet metal factory. Perhaps if I raised the screen and blasted him with the proper Pantera cut he'd raise one fisted talon and fall right in with the percussive attack, woodpeckers being your original head-bangers.

If I understand the experts correctly, our woodpecker chose the "substrate" of our woodshed roof on the basis of its resonant qualities. I have this vision of him approaching the shed for the first time, tapping it gently, then inclining his little woodpecker ear and blinking as he appraises the tone and reverberation, not unlike any number of musicians I've watched plucking around in the guitar store. Perhaps he believes the corrugations channel the sound, projecting it further down-valley where all the single woodpecker ladies live. He chose well, as the racket can be heard all over the farm and even beneath a pillow.

We're at the time when we need to restock the woodshed. I hope we won't disturb his groove too badly. I trust if he really loves the sound of the place he'll be willing to work around us. Last year he (or one of his relatives) chose the conical galvanized roof of our old wire corn bin located out behind the granary, which at least gave us some sonic buffer.

Of course the whole production is more entertaining than irritating, and I wish the woodpecker luck. It is my understanding that in addition to soliciting a mate, he is staking out territory (there is overlap), and if he is moved to so do so by creating a one-note symphony akin to someone shooting a fully-automatic BB gun at a pole barn, who am I to question? Is this not the courting technique that allowed his ancestors to outlast all those other dinosaurs? "Good for him," I think as I step out into the fresh spring morning only to be greeted by a sound like a 55-gallon drum rolling through a hailstorm. Love is in the air, and in fact cannot be avoided.

PLANTING BEFORE THE RAIN

Despite an ongoing prevalence of chickens, ours is not a farm in the professional sense, but I was nonetheless under some pressure this spring to get the crops in. (OK, *crop,* singular.) But still one must till! (OK, scratch up a half-acre patch and scatter it with canola seed upon which plants we will graze the chickens.)

But: *farming.*

The main pressure with farming is weather. On the day I chose to plant, we had been in a sustained dry stretch but I was confident it would rain by midweek. I retain this predictive ability after being raised by people of the soil whose livelihoods depended on keeping an eye to the sky, an ear to the wind, and a mind on the moon lest the hay get wet or the seeds not sprout. Also I know my zip code and how to spell weather.com.

At noon the radar showed nothing but clear skies, but the hourly forecast had heavy rain coming in just prior to suppertime—then nothing but dry weather for another week. In other words, to get that good sprouting boost, those seeds had to go in that day. At midafternoon my wife started moving the chicken fence while I fueled the tractor, a smallish unit belonging to my mother-in-law and equipped with a rear-mounted tiller. By the time I had greased the tiller and outlined the perimeter of the patch, the kids were home from school and I realized I probably wasn't going to get done in time to beat the rain. I recruited my teenaged daughter (who's been driving the tractor for years now) to finish the tilling while I got the seed and fetched the broadcaster. My wife helped me with the per-acre math calculations, while the younger daughter helped by gathering eggs and doing her other chores without supervision. We are—I like to think —a normal family in that we have some grouching in our growing, and our dance of life is not without trodden toes, but we do know how to work together, even if everyone is not whistling (Dad being the least whistle-y of all).

As my elder daughter churned the dandelions, I tromped the tilled swathes with the broadcaster slung from my shoulder, scattering seeds across the upturned dirt. By the time we finished, clouds were sliding in.

And then it didn't rain. Suppertime came. Nothing. My wife and elder daughter departed for a meeting in town. The roads were dry. My younger daughter and I pulled up the local radar. It showed a wall of dense rain falling across our county, but an inexplicable split centered right over our farm was leaving us untouched. We read a book, she got ready for bed. Nary a drop.

And then, just at teeth-brushing time, down it came. A roof-roaring, deck-pelting, splattery downpour. Ten minutes and it was gone, the countryside greened and glistening in the gloaming. After the child was abed I went out to close up the coop, stood a moment in the darkness, and ever so faintly from the earth, heard the rain seeping to the seed.

OFF HOURS BAR

It had been a trying couple of days, so I went to the bar. It being noon-ish, the bar was closed. Fortunately, I have a long-standing relationship with the bartender, and when I knocked and pressed my face to the glass, he paused in his pre-opening ritual, unlocked the door, and let me in. I chose a stool, put my feet on the rail, propped my elbows, and took a pull at the coffee I had brought with me. I have never had an alcoholic drink in my life and didn't intend to start on a random Monday lunch hour. But go to the bar? Sure.

I had a fifteen-minute interim before I had to drive myself to the airport and fly off for a week of driving a rental car, and what I wanted for that fifteen minutes was to settle my mind. There were other options. I could have taken a walk along the river. Meditated in the park. Sat in the pickup truck and listened to old country music songs. But in light of the week preceding and the week to come, what I really wanted was some sense of separation. Of stopping time. Of playing hooky from real life. And no better place for that than a well-worn tavern on a sunny spring day.

The place smelled like last decade's cigarettes and good

slopped beer, and the wooden floor creaked as the bartender went around slinging fresh coasters on the side tables. It was dark in there, of course, in the best velvet molasses sort of way, the dimness providing its own shelter, especially contrasted as it was by the fresh spring sunlight visible through the two street-side windows. When the bartender slid back the glass and the sound of traffic filtered in through the screens, it was as comforting as any white noise waterfall machine, a soundtrack heightening the sense that here in the pub life stood still as everyone else hustle-bustled.

And so I sat, a lifelong non-smoking teetotal surrounded by the nicotine patina of a shopworn juke joint, feeling plumb peaceful. We all have our sanctums, and one of mine is an off-hour bar. The latent energy of loud music and loud stories and loud drinkers has retreated into the old walls and behind the still bottles, leaving in the silence a feeling that the second hand is not sweeping.

Among my accidental achievements in this life I count the accumulation of panic holes like this empty bar. A place where you've earned the right of entry and the right of just sitting there, no questions asked. I talked with the bartender a little; desultory stuff, offhand stuff, easy stuff. He—even off-duty—dropped into that seasoned barkeep mode of listening and answering but not pressing, and I enjoyed my coffee, but I also just sat there, my truck keys and money clip and reading glasses off to one side, unnecessary during this tiny stretch of real-life recess.

Then it was time to go, and I did. Halfway to the airport I realized I'd left my reading glasses on the bar. I smiled, knowing they were under good care, and it would be necessary for me to fetch them upon my return.

YOUNG AUTHORS

The conga line was no longer a line, but rather a fluid knot of nearly a thousand happy children winding in and around itself throughout the aisles of the auditorium while Cyril Paul and the Calypso Monarchs played from the stage. Cyril himself—in his 80s now—took a turn to dance with the youngsters, and it was tough to imagine how they would possibly settle back into their seats, but moments after Cyril struck the drumhead a final beat, they were all quietly in place, clutching their notebooks and directing their eyes toward the podium, where the chief organizer welcomed them to a young author's conference. After her remarks, she invited me to deliver the keynote speech. I began by assuring the kids I was not there to be cool and hip, as I am a dad with bad hair over fifty. This always gets a laugh and has the added advantage of being true. Then, just to set the standard, I showed them a slide of my third grade report card, in which my teacher quite rightly expressed reservations about my future. Then I talked about writing, and then I ended by showing a three-second video of my neighbor blowing up a silo with his homemade cannon, because you want the kids to appreciate art.

Then the young ones dispersed for a day of workshops. I attended one of these, taught by a man named Joe Horton. "I'm a rapper, an author, and a professor," he said by way of introduction. He is also a husband and father, so he grinned and added, "And a trash-taker-outer." The kids giggled at that.

Using a combination of lecture, conversation, guided visualization, and a writing exercise, Horton wove those children a lovely fifty minutes about the mystery of creativity, pictographs, the birth of language, Northeastern African history, vintage graffiti in the Roman Colosseum, and how our strength and intelligence as humans arise from our differences. When he asked the children for their thoughts, hands shot up, and ideas poured forth. When he asked them to write, the room filled with the rustle and scratch of every single pencil to paper, no goading required. Nor any reward, save the writing itself.

I gave my address four mornings in a row. Each day I looked out and saw hundreds and hundreds of engaged, attentive, bright-eyed children of all colors and creeds. That is not a slogan, that is not a hope, that is a fact. Their energy and their intelligence were a live force in the room. It was my privilege to be among them. It will be my privilege to step aside and let them pass me by. I am getting more and more cranky about folks who want to fight the future in fear. Here is your beautiful, hopeful America, I thought, as I watched them all dance. "Find the rhythm!" cried Cyril as the children serpentined, hands-to-shoulders in a single joyful chain, "Find the root of the song!"

They are the root of the song.

CHIVE BLOSSOMS

The chive blossoms hit their peak last week and remain a lovely purple, although they've shaded to the pale side after three days of rain. Today, however, the sun is out and the bees are at the buds, even the plants laid flat by all the precipitation. It's good to see the bees.

A guy shouldn't get into the idea of favorite plants when he lives in the north, eager as we are to see any green shoot cracking the freeze-dried earth, but chives are right up there, coming on early and good to eat the minute they're long enough to pluck, chop, and sprinkle. Or chew up right there on the spot, give yourself some fresh onion breath well before the first lawn is mowed.

There was a time I raised a lot of herbs, and I miss that. Miss plucking flavor from the back yard. Right now I'm in one of those stretches where it's just enough to keep the bills paid and get the kids raised. What green food we have is thanks to my wife, who just yesterday planted thyme, for which I am grateful. She also raises wheelbarrows full of garlic that will save your soul from spoiling and in a pinch can double as softballs.

A long time ago I read a gardening book that recommended the use of chive blossom vinegar. I believe the author invoked the term *infusion*, which, like the term *chiffonade*, you can trot out when you need to fake-book some foodie. Basically what you do is fill a jar with chive blossoms, drown them in vinegar, then use the vinegar, which now has—is *infused* with—a mild onion-y flavor.

It really is simple, and it really is good. And most magically, the blossoms turn the vinegar a divine pink. The pink doesn't last, but the feeling you'll get when you first see it—so pure, so surprising—will. They say you shouldn't expose the jar to sunlight, but I have to, at least for a day or two, just for the beauty of the tincture.

My daughters indulge me by helping with the annual chive blossom vinegar tradition. It's an easy one, requiring all of fifteen minutes to snip the plants, rinse the flowers, and stuff the jar. Some years we remember to heat the vinegar, some years we don't. Go ahead and knock off half a star. You might find a pickled bug in there too. Bonus protein. Restore that half a star.

After a week or two of steeping, we'll pour the vinegar off into a slim glass bottle with a porcelain stopper. (One year we stuffed the blossoms one by one down the neck of that bottle. It looked so pretty and food-magaziney, then we realized there was no good way to fish the blossoms out.) We store the bottle in the pantry, in the dark, and come winter when we shake it over fries or fish or any other dish, the pink has faded but still blossoms with the warm flavor of sun.

SUMMER LIGHT

Outside my window the June evening is winding down and the sunlight is goldening and the shadows are winning the lawn and the birdsongs are of the settling sort. The leaves are the lushest they'll be all season, the greens green without reservation, the down-valley landscape fresh-grown and broccoli-shouldered. A strand of spider-silk strung from the cherry tree shifts between silver and invisible at the whim of the breeze.

Earlier, a spotted fawn gangled through the yard.

When my nine-year-old daughter came home from the last half-day of school this noon, I met her at the mailbox and we walked the driveway together. She was of two minds about the moment: Giddy at the prospect of the unfettered afternoon and summer to follow, but teary about leaving her teacher and classroom in the past, and even more so over a friend who would be moving away. There wasn't much to say, other than to simply review and acknowledge the facts. You clear the third grade, you're not buying platitudes.

We sat beside each other on the front porch steps for a while, then got a snack.

As a parent, I am a parent: regularly confused, underqualified, overreactive, jittery, and for the rest of it just fetch your thesaurus and work from what I've given you. On the upside, my children send me to the metaphorical mirror on a regular basis, where out of basic responsibility I examine my motives and actions and rate of follow-through and then resume with fresh—if not firm—resolve. When you are doing for others, you just have to do better.

But still you wobble. In your heart, if not your feet. I regularly make the mistake of reading the news, a habit akin to repeatedly prying the lid off the septic tank for a morbid peek, then, in a rush to replace it, dropping the lid on my big toe. One limps away, unsettled by the idea that dodging bad happenings, like dodging asteroids, is largely a matter of dumb luck. And you with a child to raise.

And so when given a world as beautiful as this little patch was at end of day, I hardly know what to do with it other than try to take it in and maybe even type it up. By now day has gone to gloaming, and a single robin is steadily piping. The young one is in bed, reading a book with her mother. In a moment I will leave the desk and wander down to close up the chicken coop. After our snack my daughter and I walked down there hand-in-hand to collect the eggs. The sun was still high in the sky. I touched her hair and it was warm. In the basket, the eggs were light brown and dark brown and white and aqua-green. Just now down by the old barn I spied my first firefly. There is not much to do but cherish the light when you have it.

TERMINAL MOWER

Last year I wrote a column about our old riding lawn mower and how it served us well, though it clattered near death. I now regret to report the clatter may have become a death rattle.

It had a good run. We bought it shortly after moving to the farm. A few hundred bucks, I think. Just your basic off-brand rider, no bagger, nothing fancy, simply serviceable. The previous owner was storing it in our shed, and when she offered it for sale I pursed my lips, then unpursed them long enough to rattle off some high-toned declaration about how when I was a kid on the farm we *pushed* the mower and were it not for all the pushing we would have become low-level gumption-deficient criminals on the lam with atrophic calves. I may have furthermore harrumphed and said By God.

I hung in there for longer than was sensible, leaning into that push mower like some sweaty Sisyphus of the switch-grass, simultaneously mowing down clover and common sense. I would knock the last strip flat, turn to draw a forearm across my brow and survey my accomplishment, only to get boosted in the butt by the grass roaring back. I swear sometimes it sprouted and went to seed in the time it took me to make a lap.

Understand: This is not some gorgeous putting green situation. Our yard is a potholed ramble of molehills, dandelions and encroaching burdock. I'm anticipating the letters about "oh just let it go to prairie," but what we're talking here is an essential fire break for the buildings and general pest and tick control for picnics. Also, one wishes to be able to locate the children, especially those just visiting. I have no yard pride, but I do like to walk around without a machete.

Then there came a day when in a pinch I consented to borrow the rider down in the shed. After a seated landscape commute that resolved itself in less than two hours, we made an offer on the rider and it was ours.

Now it has logged untold acreage, and looks it. Somewhere along the line the plastic hood and side shrouds became detached and then lost, so we just mowed hoodless, rat-rod style. Mice packed the space around the air cleaner with grass and feed bag fragments, which smell funny when hot. The left front tire held air just long enough to finish the job. The mow deck cut at an angle, creating a serrated look to the lawn that in the right hands could be used to artistic ends but instead just brings to mind a bad day at the barbershop. Once I dropped the front end into a rut and hit a wooden fencepost with such force that a plume of black smoke burped out the exhaust, and while I'm certain I cracked the block, I found that as long as I topped off the oil every now and then, all was well. Or, survivable.

But then last month the assistant gardener (to whom I may or may not be related) overran an unidentified object of sufficient size and consistency to blow off all the belts and bend the understructure to the point that my mechanical abilities are exceeded. Today I loaded the mower into the back of the pickup. Tomorrow I take it to the mower doctor for a verdict. Hopes are low.

In the meantime, a fellow came by with a zero-turn and mowed the whole works in a trice for a reasonable price. I can already feel my character weakening. So much so that when my wife suggested we call him a second time, I couldn't even summon the energy to harrumph.

CHICKEN BUCKET

I have just dumped the chicken bucket, for which the chickens will thank me later. Here in the moment their gratitude is obscured by their behavior, intermittently visible through a cloud of dust and feathers as the birds peck and scratch and steal and snatch—and that's before they even get to the vittles.

For those non-fowlers among you, it is important that I distinguish the chicken bucket from the feed bucket. Each morning when I turn the chickens out, I dip into a 55-gallon drum beside the run and distribute a nice mix of grains and crumbles, which they attack with similar Visigothian verve. After this initial rush, the birds disperse to the rest of the pen, where salad resides in the form of insects and succulent canola plants. The pen itself is made of portable netting, which I move every few days to replenish said salad.

So: diverse grains and fresh greens. Plenty to eat, and all day to eat it. And yet whenever I show up with the chicken bucket it is as if the chickens have spent the previous week staked to three square feet of the barren Mojave.

It's not like the food in the chicken bucket leads the list of your high-grade poultry foods. In fact, the bucket (plastic, formerly containing ice cream, and stored beneath the kitchen sink) is a reservoir of all we reject: moldy bread, dehiscent peppers, browned avocados, beef bones, pan-scrapings, scape snippings, clotty milk, rancid nuts, fuzzy unidentifiables, lettuce-trimmings, and pretty much anything else, including egg shells and sometimes *actual chicken bits*.

And they go after it like it's the last cheese curd at the Packers game.

If the weather is nice and I have the time, I enjoy doling out the chicken bucket contents—the *solid* contents, anyway—one item at a time. It's fun to fling a bit of biscuit to the far end of the run and watch the flock converge on it in a cyclone of feathers, then sling some ham fat in the other direction and giggle as the birds surge toward it in a cackling stampede. Then, when I've cherry-picked the last solid bits, I tip out the rest and it's like someone smashed a piñata in a prison riot. *Lord of the Flies* for the backyard chicken set. And cheaper than cable.

In the past I have declared that chickens are simply pigs with feathers. I stand by that statement, and you would too, if you had a chicken bucket. Neither hogs nor hens are particularly possessed of good manners, especially when there is disgusting grub at hand. But in the end, the chickens are more consistent in their gratitude. Oh, I like a good pork chop, and *Oh!* bacon. But your well-bucketed chicken—once it is done rabidly pecking—will drop a thank you daily, and as you watch the yolk turn a deep yellow-orange in the pan, its own golden sun in a nimbus of white, you turn to chuck the shell into the bucket beneath the sink, ponder the swill within and understand: food runs a circle, nutrition is unnerving, and life is good.

Thank goodness.

GENE LOGSDON

The year-end celebrity death roundups will fail to note, but we have lost the contrary farmer, Gene Logsdon. Fortunately he leaves for us an accumulation of books (including *The Contrary Farmer*) and other writings so highly stacked it would jam the beaters of a medium-sized manure spreader, an image to which I believe he would not object. After all, this is a man who wrote a book called *Holy Sh*t* only without the asterisk. He ran into difficulty during promotional tours for that one because they wouldn't let him say the title on the radio, a truly stinky irony when you consider all the other things you might hear on the radio. When my wife and I were revving up to raise our own pigs, I spent a lot of time studying Gene's instructive *All Flesh Is Grass*, and in fact kept it handy in the bathroom. I sent him a photo of the book beside the toilet, and he got a charge out of that.

My wife and I visited Gene and his wife Carol at their Ohio farm once. For me this was a true celebrity moment, as I still remember reading Gene's column in the *Farm Journal* when I was a kid. Gene would have barked with laughter at my awe, as he was the least star-like fellow. Instead he took us tromping around the acreage and put me at my ease with stories about corn pickers and buck sheep.

For a while Gene and I traded letters. I re-read them this week. We shared our thoughts on irrigation, lambing, country music, talk radio, chickens, religion, catalpa tree fence posts, pig fences, and writing. For all the fine farming advice Gene gave me (and the world) I think it was those conversations centered around our shared (and largely accidental) work as self-employed writers I cherished most. We were both surprised and delighted to be allowed to type for our supper, and to meet someone else who approached it with agrarian intent: Just put on your boots and keep shoveling (the metaphor extends itself). In fact, Gene's output shamed mine: I had been whining about some authorial struggle when my wife pointed to a list of Gene's books, and said, "He's writing the *pants* off you!

Gene also out-farmed me. I've dabbled, but over time other pursuits have reduced me to running a few chickens, and I haven't had pigs now for some years. But I still read Gene's work. His *Small-Scale Grain Raising* is sown with far more than planting advice. As an admirer of both men, I nonetheless like to think that Gene Logsdon—with his earthiness, his happy cussedness, his prose a reflection of his twinkling eyes, his willingness to bull forward between moments of reflection—was Wendell Berry for us sinners and underachievers skulking around there in the back pews.

Finally, as I look at my wife and the lines I have put on her face, I close with respect for Carol, who knew the writer and the farmer as the man he was.

DEER STRIKE

Thirty-five years with a Wisconsin drivers license and against all prodigious odds I have never hit a deer.

[*PAUSE, while writer goes down to pole barn and knocks on a whole pile of wood.*]

OK, we're back. Yah. Never hit a deer.

Now then. I have been hit *by* a deer. Twice. First time was a couple years back. Only brand new car we've ever owned. I was traveling down a long hill at full double-nickels when a doe flashed out of the ditch weeds at a right angle to my direction of travel and went head-first into the rear driver's side door. There followed a terrific *whomp*, and when I got the car stopped I anticipated the worst, but when I did the walk-around there was no deer to be found and the car was impeccable save for a trout-fly's worth of whitetail hair wedged in a seam between the wheel well and rear quarter-panel. I assume what you had there was a testimony to luck, plastics, and borrowed time. Whatever, it's the kind of mystery I accept happily and without question.

I drove on.

Then last month I made a run to the neighbor's place

after dark. I was driving our 1994 Chevrolet Silverado plow truck, a sturdy beast of long duration and decent sheet metal and equipped with a radio that glows green while it plays old country music after dark, which whups your podcast any day, and I will admit to you that I was taking full advantage of the posted legal limit and Waylon was goin' full-tilt boogie when a deer emerged in the adjacent lane moving at the same tempo, and in the time it took to register on my retina, dove directly toward the truck. In the instant I eased to the right a touch, but having responded to more than one ambulance call in which someone tried to swerve around a deer and got the worst of it, I didn't jerk the wheel, and the deer made impact just behind the front left wheel. There followed not a *whomp* but a *WHAM!* and then a second *WHAM!* The second *WHAM!* transpired a door's-thickness from my left shoulder and made me sit up real straight, in fact I may have given myself a spontaneous chiropractic adjustment.

I regret to report the deer did not thrive. For that matter, neither did the truck. By the light of my cellphone I could see there had been extensive damage done, but by the light of the following morning I discovered that the damage stretched from front to back, caving the front quarter panel, the door, and the bedside panel. Furthermore the mirror was shattered and bent around backward.

As the truck is accidentally insured, I took it to the body shop. By the time the appraiser finished, his clipboard was sagging. Then he tallied up an estimate, which, if approved as submitted, will allow me to purchase my first Tesla. In the interim, I rumble along in our rumpled Silverado, my window down three inches (won't go down any farther now due to the deer dent), the old green-glow radio playing as I drive my zero-deer-hit streak into its thirty-sixth year.

Knock-knock.

TOM AND THE BRUSH HOG

It was good to visit my neighbor Tom this week. It had been too long. I can see his shed from my ridge—it's just a shade under two miles as the crow flies, and not much farther by road—but I hadn't been over there for months. In fact, our last communication was by old-fashioned mail. I had been in another state giving lessons to young students about writing, and I concluded each talk with a video of Tom toppling a concrete silo by blasting it with his homemade cannon. So delighted was the children's reaction I took the time in the motel room later to jot a note to Tom describing their joy and letting him know how he was helping to shape young minds via homemade artillery. Art is sometimes ballistic.

So when the brush hog busted, I figured I might wind up at Tom's. It wasn't a major situation. The nut on the bolt that holds the bracket that secures the top link had come loose and untwisted itself unnoticed (that the operator did not notice this may negatively affect his performance review but that is another discussion) and when things came undone the cutting height of the machine could no longer be properly controlled. I was able to replace the nut and bolt easily enough, but in doing so realized that an essential part—a hollow tube that sheathed the bolt so it wouldn't wear through—had gone missing. The sheath (drawing on my agricultural mechanics background I identified it as a "collar") had to be a specific length, diameter, and bore. I had nothing in my shed that would do, and an online search of the local farm, hardware and big box stores yielded nothing even close. So I did what I should have done in the first place: Threw the bolt and bracket into the car, and headed for Tom's place.

Tom had visitors. He was showing them photos of his car, which was recently stolen and crashed. He has a whole presentation worked up. After he finished, I showed him the bolt and bracket and explained that I need a collar for it. Neither Tom nor his visitors seemed to understand. I explained again. Then one of the visitors, a fellow whom I happen to know is familiar with mechanical things said, "Oh, you mean a *bushing*," and I have just enough farm fixit in my background to know he was right, which may have explained why my online search yielded nothing and I am the guy writing newspaper columns.

Then it was out to Tom's shop, which is not a straight-line trip as one is continually diverted by eight decades of stories. Eventually we found ourselves rooting around in the iron repository, a clanging heap of oddments located in the general vicinity of the twenty-ton press. Shortly one of the visitors located a steel pipe of the exact bore and diameter I needed. It was too long, but we quickly cut it to length, and I was back in business.

We shot the breeze then, as one does, but I had work waiting at home, so when Tom got going on his homemade tractor-mounted snow blower—a story I love (especially the part about how it shoots snow over a two-story house) but have heard before—I thanked Tom for the part and the visitors for their help and headed home. Down in the shed everything bolted up just perfect, and I set off for the back forty. I was happy to have fixed the brush hog on the cheap, but even happier when I hit the ridge, looked over toward Tom's shed, and knew he was still there with his tools, his steel, and his stories.

NORB'S COOP

I just spent three days writing in a chicken coop and completing the final draft of a play. Both are new experiences.

I've never really felt like I required a special place in which to write. This sentiment arises in part from my having never once heard my brother the logger say he needs a special place to sharpen his saw, and we are both in the business of converting trees. Mostly I simply believe in getting the work done in the space available (in fact this entire column is being typed in the passenger seat of a 2002 Toyota minivan running Highway 29 for three hours not counting bathroom breaks). But when given the opportunity to rearrange words in amenable surroundings, I know enough to be grateful—and get to work.

And so when the organization Write On, Door County gave me the opportunity to weave into one of my small self-employment yapping tours a visit of their facilities and spend some time working in Norb Blei's old chicken coop up there in Door County, I did so with thanks.

Unless the experience is lost to my ever-expanding collection of memory holes, I don't believe I ever met Norb Blei.

Much of what I have learned of the legendary Door County (by way of Chicago) writer has come via excellent pieces written by Myles Dannhausen. It was thanks to Dannhausen that I was able to take my seat in Mr. Blei's old wooden chair informed about, and with proper reverence and respect for, the millions (and it was easily millions) of words that had percolated (and often boiled over) within those close wooden walls.

I got some good work done in there. My stay coincided with a gloriously breezy, sunny stretch, which meant I got to write to the tune of my favorite soft symphony: summer sounds through an open screen. There were disruptions, of course. Specifically, a hummingbird, two spotted fawns, and a persistent gopher. And I did have to struggle back to civilization at least twice a day for fresh coffee. But each time I flagged, or was tempted to bug out and check the news, I looked at the varnish on the low table before me, and knew it had the sort of shine that only comes from a pair of elbows regularly applied, and I got back to work.

This play I'm working on is an adaptation of a book I wrote some time ago. Among other challenges I am most daunted by the fact that I have to cut eighty percent of the words in the book in order to fit it to stage time (lest I trigger a wave of numb butts and narcolepsy). But then "daunting" runs a sliding scale, and frankly comes in well below logging. So again, I was happy to be there, scrivening in a chair polished by a man who understood your number one writing tool is located at the back of your pants and only works when it's planted. Just before leaving, with a few more thousand words toward my own million, I read another piece in which Dannhausen describes Mr. Blei taking a moment to break from conversation and open the trunk of his car, in which resided copies of his books, always for sale. "The true mark of a Midwestern writer," wrote Dannhausen, "[is] a trunk full of copies of his books, ready to hustle." And that made me smile, because that's how this column ends: Me typing away while my wife drives our little family along, another mixed work/vacation trip winding down, and eight feet behind me in the rear of this old van, two cardboard boxes filled with my books—the good news being, when the trip began, there were three.

RE-TAKING OUT THE TRASH

Roughly two hours ago it occurred to me that today is the day we take out the trash and recycling. When I say, "occurred to me," I mean that is when my wife's text arrived reminding me that today is the day we take out the trash and recycling.

Taking the trash and recycling "out" is a cultural affront to me in that I was raised country, back when you took care of the trash and recycling mainly via burn barrel and pickup truck, with support from the local dump, which predated the term *landfill*. If you find this environmentally horrifying, you should know that even our local dump had rules, or at least one, that rule being if you couldn't fit it through the gate, you couldn't dump it. And this of course was an improvement on the real old days in which rural dumps were simply located "out back." Ravines were especially valued in this respect. We have one behind our old granary, where generations of farmers backed to the edge of the cut and with boot and broom sent everything tumbling down the hillside. Again, while I should perhaps be troubled by this desecration of Our Mother the Earth, I gotta say all that junk has provided great archaeological diversion for my young ones and me. It is exciting to unearth old oil cans, feed scales, and unidentified machines that look like dinosaur skeletons.

So the idea that I might have to bag my trash in a special bag and sort my recycling into specific tubs goes against my admittedly backward grain. However, I have resolved as a project of middle age to resist intransigent grumpiness over change in general, and therefore am happy to do my part to keep dish detergent out of the downstream alfalfa. And so, whenever the receptacles are brimming, we call the garbage company (no matter what euphemism may be currently in play, I'm going with "garbage," if only as a reminder to myself that I create a trail of waste) and request a pickup. This request is necessitated by our living outside the standard weekly pickup loop. If we forget to request pickup, we have to hustle our garbage down the hill to the main road, where our neighbors Denny and Linda kindly allow us to park it beside their mailbox. Perhaps they are just too polite to say no.

On holiday weeks the schedule is knocked back by a day, and let me tell you it is a rare sort of embarrassment to frantically pack all your trash down to the neighbor's mailbox only to return three hours later to find it blown all over his yard because you were off by one day. By God, back when we dumped things down the ravine this never... Oh, right —intransigence.

An hour and 55 minutes after my wife sent me that text today, I sprang into action, gathering tubs, cinching sacks, and hunting down stray tuna cans. Then I went bombing down the hill, hung a right, and headed for Denny's mailbox...only to be greeted by four mailboxes (as many as we can see on this stretch of road) each guarded by a set of empty bins.

Missed it.

There commenced a sad and fuming retreat back up the hill. On my honor, I did not back up to the ravine. Rather, I unloaded and neatly arranged the tubs so they will be ready to be taken out next week.

Should it occur to me.

HAIR BALL

The sun rose and set the dewdrops afire, the cat hacked up a hairball, and the day began.

I have this little daybreak routine: Rise, let the cats out of the doghouse (yes, I know), let the chickens out of the coop, then walk back to the house and empty the twin dehumidifiers subbing for a sump pump in the basement. On this particular morning I had completed two of three and was strolling beneath the apple tree when the fuzziest of our three cats—who had not been present for curfew the previous evening—hunched up on the sidewalk and commenced to retching.

I have never been hungover in my life and I'm not saying that cat was, but this was my first thought, and I went with it, imagining him down at the kitty tavern 'til all hours, knocking back miniature beers and teensy chasers, maybe purring at some lady kitty and nudging the catnip chews her way until he remembered he'd been fixed, at which point he retreated with his beer to the jukebox, where he slumped into more serious drinking, his pupils sad and wide in the barroom gloom, his tail limp.

You can see why sometimes it takes me a while to empty the dehumidifiers.

I myself had been out late, but only because I was riding in a tow truck near midnight, the neighbor's pickup truck having conked out on me during a trip to town for theater rehearsal and an artistic meeting happening at an artistic hour. I was driving the neighbor's truck because my truck had also conked out and was in the shop. Ultimately this played into synchronicity when I directed the tow truck driver to haul my neighbor's pickup to the same shop where my repaired pickup awaited, and thus I was able to drive myself home in my own vehicle after paying my bill at midnight. Sometimes karma arrives on a flatbed. As far as the neighbor, he is gone on vacation until next Monday, which buys me some time to frame the escapade and explain how I got his keys.

All this to say I suppose neither the cat nor I were at the top of our game right out of dawn's gate, but at least I wasn't ralphing on the sidewalk. I was, however, sleep-deprived enough that I found myself not only studying the cat as his body lurched in the cumulative rhythm inherent to the process, but *rooting* for the cat, as in, yes, you can do it, that's it, almost there...as if I was some hairball doula, midwifing the moment. When the cat finally produced a glistening grass-threaded wad of efflux that formed its own sort of dewdrop, I felt as if we had really accomplished something together.

Having unburdened himself, the cat regarded the wet lump between his paws, then padded nonchalantly off to sun himself on the porch. I emptied the dehumidifiers, then made my way to my room over the garage, where I powered up my computer and some music. First song out of the speakers was J.J. Cale singing "They Call Me the Breeze," just the way he wrote it, at an easy shuffle. The perfect speed, it

seemed, at which that cat and I might approach this
new day.

THE ART OF LAUNDRY

I drove my deer-bashed pickup truck over to a friend's house this week and we talked about art. We were hunkered in a dark room and outside the rain was falling and out the window the trees were wet and dark and we had a good decade-and-a-half of ups and downs between us, so the conversation came easily.

We're both, frankly, a couple of lunks, and nothing about either of us would appear obviously artisanal, although a couple of his tattoos might qualify, including one that doubles as a map of Wisconsin. I am tattoo-free, a matter of neither pride nor propriety but rather due to working as a nurse in my early twenties, from which stint I emerged with a lasting perception of the human body as a most mutable canvas, and thus have never been able to trust that the star-spangled tiger dragon on my bicep might not one day migrate 'round to my triceps and come to resemble a bruised and wobbling cantaloupe.

Our conversation began with old pickup trucks, in particular the fact that we both loved them and drove them but were pretty much out of luck when it came time to fix them.

This reliance on people with talents other than ours is humbling, as it ought to be. We are also blessed in that we both live rurally and thus must maintain more than a passing acquaintance with the septic tank guy, an angel of mortality if ever there was one. If you're going to work up to art, the septic tank is a good place to start.

The term *artist* is freighted with all manner of connotation, much of which leaves both of us uncomfortable. For starters, to call oneself an artist is to suggest self-anointment. Then again, that is true for any number of endeavors, including farming. There is also the idea that the artist presumes the world will be better for the dispensation of the art in question, when in fact, what might better serve the public is a bridge that doesn't fall down. Then again, over time we have both come to feel that when the only bottom line is the bottom line, somebody's gonna get buried. Art is full of foolishness and fakery and so is the rest of the world. I'll take my chances.

We also agreed that if you stand around kicking the dirt too long, you just kill the grass. If there is something that music and words and all art and hay bales share, it is that they don't do you any good just sitting there. You have to punch the clock. There will be time for parsing later. There is work in beauty, and beauty in work.

We left it at that. The rain had stopped, but the blacktop was still wet, and hissed beneath my tires. I hung one elbow out the window, and counted among my blessings the privilege of contemplation and conversation. I also noted my neighbor the farmer had gotten his second crop up before the storm.

By now the sun was out. When I bumped up our old potholed driveway there was laundry on the line. It blew like prayer flags, it was beautiful in the breeze.

TALKING TO MYSELF

Yah, that was me at the stoplight talking to myself. In my defense, I was hard at work.

Having spent the first 39 years of my life as a bachelor, I long ago got past the idea that there should be any stigma in holding conversation with the person whose social security number matches mine. By exteriorizing one's internal monologue, one provides oneself a constant—if not always agreeable—companion. So yah, I talk to myself. (Trail me long enough and you will also learn that I yell and curse at myself, but that's a different column.)

Lately, however, I've been talking to myself out loud on purpose. For the first time in years I am involved in a theatrical production as an actor and as such am forced by the director (who seems to think he is in charge) to memorize bits of lines. I say "bits" because other actors in the play have to memorize swathes, pages, and buckets of lines, whereas I'm mostly responsible for asides and interjections. Also, my main prop is a book, from which my character reads most of his lines. And yet still I stammer, falter, and deliver stemwinding "improvisations." If at any point the other actors rush me, steal the book and pummel me with it, I can't say I blame them, and that'll make for quite a scene.

Back in the day I did lots of community theater. Memorized large roles (often while sitting in a bathtub with soggy index cards). I never found an easy way to get the words lodged in my brain. Mostly I just went over the script again and again. Try a line, back up, cover it up, try it again. And again. And when that one seemed to click, move on to the next one. I could always tell I was getting closer when I stopped seeing the script as words but rather started seeing it as shapes. When I had a sense of the paragraphs as blocks with unique borders and then started seeing those blocks in a stack, then I knew I was on my way.

As of this writing, I'm almost there with this script. It's turning into shapes. Or at least it was, until this week when I reprinted it in a different format so it would fit inside my prop book. Now all of a sudden passages that were horizontal rectangles have become vertical rectangles, some of the rectangles are unexpectedly chopped off at the bottom of the page, and certain italicized stage directions have shifted or gone from one line to three. This is the actor's struggle.

In an attempt to re-implant the script geometry on my brain, I am running the lines aloud at every opportunity, including in a 1994 Chevy Silverado at a stoplight in broad daylight. And so I should clarify my opening line: What you saw there was not a man talking to himself, but rather a man perfecting his art. Yes the stage was a rolling dent-fest with a broken mirror and a tendency to stall out mid-monologue, but as William Shakespeare once said to himself, *Rectangle, rectangle, square.*

RIDING WEST

Once upon a time for the purposes of ranch work I rode the Greyhound from Eau Claire, Wisconsin, to Hanna, Wyoming. As I recall this was about a 48-hour run, although that's a suspiciously nice round number. Still, it was long enough.

I remember it now like a dated movie, the colors still rich but gone a little grainy. I was wearing jeans and a denim jacket, and had switched my tennie-runners and feathered hair for an ill-fitting cowboy hat (and boots to match) before Grandpa drove me downtown to the bus station. I remember he had a cough he couldn't shake. What I didn't know then is it was the first sign of the pulmonary fibrosis that would take him too soon, his daily walk, sit-ups and trim bearing notwithstanding.

Just now in a karmic twist, "Last Bus Home," by Enzo has cycled into my playlist so the film stock in my head takes on an ochre hue. Hour after hour, alone at the Greyhound window I squinted against the lens-flare landscape, trying to pull off a full Marlboro Man. This was difficult, as I had never had a beer, let alone a cigarette, and still attended Bible study.

The two young men in the seats behind me were from Israel. They were riding the Greyhound from New York City to Los Angeles, where—they told me with bright smiles— they hoped to "do sex on the beach." They had been on the bus for five days. Or more. I'm remembering now that this was not some straight-shot express. We stopped at a lot of small towns along two-lane highways. During a rest break somewhere in Nebraska I ate a grocery store candy bar while sitting on a sidewalk next to a guy who leaned against his backpack and talked about how he had just returned from an ill-fated expedition up Mount Aconcagua during which some of his fellow climbers lost fingers to frostbite. I remember this clearly because in one of those odd cosmic twists, only the week previous I had spoken with a high school principal in Wisconsin who had just returned from Argentina, where he had climbed Mount Aconcagua behind a group of climbers who lost their fingers to frostbite.

Shortly before we pulled into Hanna, I worked up the courage to speak with a young woman who boarded in Omaha. Her conversation was sparkling, and I remember holding myself very much at attention as one does when trying to make a good first impression even while fighting the urge to slump in despair over having not plucked up the courage to chat her up right out of Omaha. I wrote her name in a notebook and never saw her again.

The bus was slowing and I could see my boss waiting beside his Bronco. I turned to bid my two Israeli pals adieu, and looking up at me pleadingly, one of them said, "Los Angeles? We are almost there, yes?"

"Fellas," I said, with more nonchalance than I'd earned, "Yer about half way."

They sank back in despair. I stepped off the bus, worked all summer, and come August, flew back home in the space of an afternoon.

SPLITTING PUNK

On the final day of August I split firewood. The sun had all the grasshoppers snapping in the tall grass, although the other audible insects were operating at a desultory drone, as if—having passed the season of frenetic fertility—they were just playing out their shifts until the first frost hits. Indeed, the thistles had gone to seed.

It was warm enough that I was sweating pretty heavily by the time I knocked apart the third block of oak. That sounds manly enough but I should backtrack and let you know that the tree trunk in question had rotted from the center out, so I was basically chopping wooden doughnuts, which given the lay of the grain is about as challenging as slicing a celery stalk the long way.

Furthermore while I imply the image of myself as Abe swinging the cleaver from his heels, in fact I long ago traded the manual method for the hydraulic ram method, having succumbed to the sale price of a motorized splitter that exerts 25 tons of force at the tip of the blade, making short work of your knotty oak. In this case, however, because of the doughnut factor, it was quicker to whack the wood by hand than wrassle it into the automated splitter.

Finally, as long as I'm facing facts, I did not even fell this tree. It has been dead at the bend in our driveway for a few years now and I've driven by it countless times over those years thinking, *gotta cut that*, until finally my 75-year old father showed up with his chainsaw and felled it himself, because, as he said, "I need to keep moving." In my defense he has been logging for 50 years and really knows what he is doing, whereas I have sometimes *written* about logging and am never quite sure which way the tree will topple. Does the fact that I allow my 75-year old father to cut my trees make me a bad son? I prefer to think it allows him to do what he loves while inoculating me against accusations of ageism.

But now I really was busting up that firewood, and glad to be doing it. I had just emerged from a frenetic stretch of work and weird hours only to find myself in a discombobulated funk exacerbated by my catching up on current events and watching my children at play in the waning days of summer. In times of dread and ennui, you can do worse to ground yourself with a wide stance and a splitting axe. Basic tool, basic job. Pile of wood when you're done.

That oak was real wet. The punk left by the rot acts as a sponge, drawing and holding moisture. I split until it was time to shower up and head for a meeting in town. The world was still complicated, but now it held another week's worth of fuel to be fed into the stove the winter after next, by which time the wood will have cured and maybe everything will have changed but most likely we will still need to bank the fire against the cold that works all night to seep in.

RAISIN ROOSTER

Amongst our hens there is a rooster who holds his citizenship through error, as he arrived in the mail with a batch of chicks that was supposed to be females only. They say sorting day-old-chicks by sex is an art rather than a science; I believe them, am ill-equipped to criticize, and will leave them to it. That said, waking to the unexpected sound of adolescent crowing four months later is a $3.78 letdown, far more if you add up all the feed and subtract zero pending eggs. Fortunately for him, he is an exotic (thus the $3.78) and teensy feather-footed fellow of the "silkie" variety, which is to say if you stuck him on a stick you could dust with him. To this cuteness he owes his parasitic existence, because his personality is pure rooster: self-centered, vainglorious, and single-mindedly bent on loving the ladies despite a height differential that regularly leaves him short in every respect.

He is, in summary, a waste of feed. However: vocally, this rooster has distinguished himself by adding a staccato squawk to the end of his otherwise standard *cock-a-doodle-doo*, and as much as I want to harden myself against this play for character, you can't help but laugh out loud when you hear the embellishment. In fact, early on my younger daughter and I made a game in which we wait for the bird to finish his standard crow, count off a beat, then snap our fingers and point at him just as he throws on that postscript *kawk!* It may lose something in the telling but it's quite a hoot on any given Tuesday. Especially if we crow back at him just to keep him going, a neat trick predicated on his ego.

There is no sensible reason to keep this rooster on hand (I am often asked by chicken newbies if a rooster is required in order to get the hens to lay eggs, and the answer is, *coq au vin*). In fact, the hens would celebrate his ouster, what with all the amatory pratfalling. But I forgot to mention that his comb is not a red crest and instead resembles a cross between a raisin and a wad of licorice gum. When you add this to the cock-a-doodle-coda, you have the sort of cute that has enabled him to insinuate himself into my daughter's affections to a depth that rules out drastic measures or mysterious disappearances. I am well-and-truly out that $3.78 and an exponential infinity of non-metaphorical chicken scratch. It helps, of course, that when it comes to poultry ours is hardly a bottom-line operation (the rooster shares quarters with Goldie, a nine-year-old hen who hasn't lain an egg for a couple years now) and there are other variables in play including fond memories.

School is back in session now, and each day right off the bus it is the young one's duty to grab a basket and fetch the day's eggs. We went through a stretch last month where that rooster crowed in the standard manner, without the grace note. This was a grave disappointment to my daughter, but yesterday the bird was back to his old addendum, and it was nice to see her face light up at the sound of it. In reference to his comb she has named him Turd Raisin, and I don't know if you can print that in a family newspaper, but she is family, that rooster makes her giggle, and I have heard worse during so-called presidential debates, so I will happily allow the crowing to continue.

SMALL TOWN LITERATURE

If tomorrow I am offered a few million dollars for my thoughts and dreams I will accept the check and sort the trouble and taxes later. Last week, however, I was working at a lower rate and as such was more than happy to haul my book boxes to Bloomer, Wisconsin, where I told some well-worn stories and a few new ones beneath a tent pitched on the asphalt of the street adjacent to the local library, which was celebrating its centennial. The audience included a number of volunteer fire and rescue personnel with whom I used to make ambulance runs, neighbors from my childhood, and my third grade teacher, a longsuffering woman whose positive contributions to the state of my current existence are too numerous to list here but include redirecting me to the straight and narrow (I did my straying early, in part by giddily practicing bad words in the hallway beneath the coat rack) and teaching me how to properly pronounce tortilla. Having read a lot of books and considering myself precocious, I recall quite snottily telling her that 'tortilla' rhymed with 'vanilla.' She tuned me in a trice and I've been smarter ever since, although I'm still never quite sure which way to go with 'villa.'

I knew the Bloomer gig would be a quality small-town literary event when the librarian—realizing I was probably going to yap past dusk—produced a trouble light and hung it from the tent pole behind me. She furthermore electrified it using a big ol' honkin' extension cord. Librarians are all about resources.

I have read and performed my work in all manner of settings and situations including on a heavy equipment trailer, on the back of an International Harvester straight truck, in an Old Country Buffet, adjacent to a blacksmithing demonstration, standing on a piece of plywood atop a pool table in a health food store, and once—in a moment of metaphorical perfection—from within a manure spreader. This background experience came in useful in Bloomer, as I had my back to an intersection just off the main drag and had to adjust the pacing and delivery of my material to ebb and flow with the rise and fall of the jacked-up diesel four-wheelers gunning for the overpass. Poetry owes much to rhythm, which can be found in both your Power Stroke and your Duramax, in this case the perfect soundtrack.

When I was done and had sold and signed some books and shaken some hands and refreshed some acquaintances and taken a photo with the crew who put up the tent, I boxed my books and prepared to leave, but then got caught up in conversation with a man I'd never met. In truth, he got caught up in conversation with me, because after hours and hours alone, once I get my jaw jacking I find it hard to stop. He is a combat veteran and a first responder and has other responsibilities upon which civilization depends, and we talked until it was solid dark. We spoke of our affection for the rural, small-town life, but also agreed we were grateful for having been allowed to see some of the breadth of the world. The added perspective sows healthy questions, a hedge against the certainty that leads to curdled thinking. Right at the end he spoke firmly but humbly of his duties as a citizen, a husband, and a father, and when I finally let him go and pointed the car for home and the lttle family of my own, I was tempted to reflect upon the evening and draw grand conclusions, but then simply decided to focus on the road ahead, keep driving, and keep trying.

VOLLEYBALL DAD

I like to think of myself as roughneck scribe of rugged cut and poetic intent, but right now that is difficult as I am typing up this column in the middle seat of a minivan en route to a high school volleyball game where I will be just another bald dad thinking, "*Wow that popcorn smells good,*" and perhaps peeking at my phone to check the score of the football game.

I'm happy to attend. In the day-to-day I mostly keep to myself and these games draw me out into the open where I meet other parents, even if only in passing, or to celebrate a nice spike. But this leads to a nod down at the gas station or at the post office and it is through such moments that community connections are made, common ground is found.

Of course, school athletics do not always lead to happy unification. The first time I attended a volleyball game as a parent, I dreaded it, having heard tales of overzealous sport parents exhibiting and inciting all manner of bad behavior. And indeed, five minutes into the first match between seventh graders a fellow five rows behind me began berating one of the kids on the opposing team by name, loudly criticizing her effort at every turn. I turned to get a look at him, and based on his T-shirt and ball cap logos realized he was a visiting parent yelling at one of his own kids. I turned to watch the game again but had a hard time focusing, my shoulders tensing more and more each time he hollered. I thought it was shameful, the way he was behaving, and wondered what kind of adult can't control himself in a setting such as this where the children are just learning, and then he yelled again, and before I knew what was happening, I whirled around and snapped, "Take it down a notch there, Spanky!"

Just as immediately I whirled back to face the game, my eyes wide with surprise at myself and my skin all busted out in a cold sweat. The sweat was half fear — I kept expecting him to come piling down the bleachers after me — and the other half was embarrassment. Minutes into my first game as a parent and I was already getting swept up into accosting strangers. I was *that kind of adult.*

He didn't hit me. Nor did he stop yelling. But there was a definite reduction in his tone and frequency. I call it a win.

Although I loved competing in athletics when I was my child's age, I recall having reservations about the whole "sports teach you about life" thing.

Indeed, for many young people not blessed with calf pens to clean every Saturday morning, sports provide a valuable opportunity to become acquainted with the benefits of teamwork and a solid work ethic.

In sport's purest form you are rewarded for working harder. Although even in my teens I picked up on another true life lesson of sports: if you're really good at something, the rules have wiggle room.

The bottom line is, my wife and I are grateful for the way our child has responded to being pushed beyond her comfort zone by her coaches and peers. This being an "away" game, there won't be as many of us in the stands tonight, but it will be good to see the familiar faces, to support the younger generation in the game of life and I resolve to call no stranger Spanky.

BOILED DINNER

As the last of the green drained from the field corn a cold wind scraped the first yellow leaves across the sidewalk, by reflex I decided to make boiled dinner.

First I chunked an onion. Shucked the chunks into petals and dropped them into a steel pot, then laid upon this redolent mattress a twin set of smoked ham hocks. Added water, a grinder twist or two of fresh pepper. Brought the whole works to a high boil, then backed it off to a low boil. Let it go an hour before pulling it from the stove, then, after it cooled, placed the pot in the fridge overnight. I have this theory that it helps for the hocks to rest and regroup. I have this theory, but I do not have a cooking show.

The following day I placed the ham hock and its jellied broth within a crock pot, which I set to warm while I did further chunking: carrots, potatoes, rutabagas, one white turnip, and a parsnip. The last two items were included under protest, as Mom never put them in her boiled dinner, but as my wife seemed to imply when she placed them on the cutting board, "They were on sale and I am not your mother."

There is a reason I want to make it just like Mom made it:

Boiled dinner is edible nostalgia. Just as much as I want to eat it, I want to leave the house and return a few hours later to step in from the porch and into the aroma of it, to stand at the kitchen window and listen to the quiet *lup-lup* of it working in the pot, the perfect background noise for observing autumn, the perfect time transporter back to the farmhouse warmth of our old Monarch woodstove. (In a Twitter exchange with the eminent sociologist Tressie McMillan Cottom, Ph.D., I learned that "putting on the neckbone pot" is the nostalgic Southern equivalent in nearly all respects.)

But of course I'll never make it like Mom made it. She was in possession of secret ingredients including love, history, and Dad dragooning us into loading an entire side-racked hay wagon with firewood before we came in to eat *hungry*. So if parsnips are provided, in they go, and sometimes I add celery. I do have my limits: when someone in my house suggested I substitute corned beef I said well what you have just described is boiled dinner stripped of its soul.

Last, I add cabbage. You don't want it to get soggy, at least not on the first go-round. Then I leave the house to do some chores, some outside work, try to move around in the crisp air and colors to establish contrast for that moment when we sit before the bowl and inhale the steam conveying the spirit of the dish. And then it's eat, and eat some more, and maybe even just a teensy ladle of thirds, and later after the dishes are done and the crock pot has cooled, I place it in the refrigerator, where overnight in the darkness the smoke of those hocks will infuse itself even more deeply into the dish, and when I heat a bowl for tomorrow's lunch, I will reaffirm my belief that with boiled dinner leftovers is where it begins.

JACKKNIFE JACKPOT

Life is a crapshoot and I am up two jackknives.

Yesterday we got rid of our old couch. I hated to see it go as it had a late 1940s—early 1950s vibe, but it was clad in fabric the texture of a scouring pad and I can tell you from having slept on it a night or two it was of similar comfort. So when some friends moved and their nicer, newer couch became available, we decided to donate the old couch to a local community theater, where it can make onstage appearances as a period piece prop as if some middle-aged man of the 2000s had never sat on it with a bag of Funyuns to watch Packers games on a flat screen.

I recently lost a pager. As my wife and I lugged the old couch across the living room it occurred to me we should make one last check of it in the event the pager had slipped away unnoticed during a particularly disappointing third-and-long situation. I'm not talking here about lifting up the cushions for a peek; I'm talking about blindly pushing our hands into the sofa's deepest recesses, those mysterious folds far beyond upholstery. Even in a couch of your own people, it feels kinda hinky.

But we made quite a haul.

Pony tail holders came in at an easy number one. This is no surprise, as I live in a house with three long-haired ladies. There were also bobby pins, ribbons, clips, and an array of follicular fasteners beyond my recognition. Two large magnets. A pair of serrated craft shears. Perhaps a Funyun. Enough pens and pencils to cover the school supplies for a family of five. Two bracelets and two necklaces.

And a jackknife!

I use the exclamation points because I had given up on that one. It's a simple, relatively inexpensive stainless steel paraframe number with a pocket clip (that is not foolproof, thus a jackknife in the couch), but I like it. Like it so much that when I gave it up for lost the last time (I'd lost it and found it before) I bought a replacement. As we finished excavating and loaded the couch into our pickup I patted the pair of knives clipped side-by-side to my jeans and felt like I'd won the everyday lottery.

After delivering the furniture to the theater group, I returned to work in my little office over our garage. I have a decrepit green chair in there of roughly the same style and vintage as that old couch. Although I'd already pulled the cushion to check for the pager, in light of the trove we pulled from that couch it occurred to me that I might want to do a deeper dive. And the very first thing I pulled out? Another jackknife. Of the exact same model as the other two.

Turns out I lost and replaced that jackknife twice, but only remembered it once. Absentmindedness, culminating in early Christmas. Call it chance, coincidence, or destiny if you're feeling grand, which indeed I was as I arranged all three on my desk like a king admiring his many scepters and also thinking maybe I ought to make a run to the gas station for some Funyuns and a scratch-off.

DECELERATION

I like it when my book tours take me to Oconomowoc, Wisconsin, if only to hear New York City-based publicists try to pronounce Oconomowoc. I usually allow them two or three tries before gently guiding them through it, just one of those subtle reminders to the East Coasters that out here in the Heartland we too are capable of esoterica.

I am just returned to our farm after a week that took me to several different Wisconsin venues: an auditorium in Reedsburg, the Thrasher Opera House in Green Lake, a conference room in Madison, and independent bookstores in Watertown and the aforementioned Oconomowoc. As this was a homegrown book and music tour not involving Manhattan publicists, there was no need to hand out pronunciation guides.

Now I am back in the room over the garage where I do most of my typing, and as so often happens, I find myself wanting to acknowledge the diverse blessings of these little trips. For instance, at one of the stops I met a man named Richard who once sent me a letter suggesting that the Little Library concept (in which private citizens erect birdhouse-like mini-libraries and stock them with books for the taking and trading) be extended to taverns. This seems like a fine idea to me. Imagine the glory of reading a dog-eared novel beneath the neon glow and within arm's reach of a gallon of pickled eggs! Let us have a well-read citizenry, and let them have a beer.

At another event, a woman told me she ditched her dentist appointment in order to make it to the bookstore over the noon hour. I hope she brushed twice as long that day. In another instance a woman came through the line with two books—one of mine to sign, and the other a mystery written by an acquaintance I've not seen for a long while. This woman would not have known of my familiarity with the other writer, nor will she know how in that moment she allowed me an unexpected and lovely vicarious memory visit with him.

One night last week a guitar player and I crossed Wisconsin from midnight to 3 a.m. Over one stretch between Montello and Mauston, it seemed we dodged a deer every 500 yards. The guitar player comes to the Midwest via a Connecticut childhood, a Yale education, and a long stretch of Texas roadhouses and honky-tonks. As you might expect, she is a conversationalist of the highest order. Among other things we discussed *Pedagogy of the Oppressed*, intersectionality, beef sticks, and the composition of set lists. The miles sped by and we missed all the whitetails. That segment of the tour was only three days ago, but now as my van cools in the garage it seems three years.

There is always that moment when you come in off the road—even from a mini-tour like this—and feel both happily home and disoriented. Even as I sort through the recent memories and images and flashes of a hundred brief conversations, I'm also thinking about tonight's chicken chores, tomorrow's deadlines, and catching up on the day-to-day news with my little family. There is a feeling that I am back where I belong but still decelerating. So many miles, so many faces, now I'm at my desk, going nowhere. If I offered sentiments commensurate to my situation, I would never write any other words but *thank you*.

BIRTHDAY BOTS

Five years ago I had a couple of hours to fill while my daughter was at an appointment in town, so I went to my longtime coffee shop hangout to do some writing. I first frequented the establishment in the early 1990s. Back then I was a long-haired wannabe poet living on fresh angst and café mochas. Now I read more poetry than I write, the mochas go straight to my waist so I stick to plain black coffee, I reserve my angst for the electric bill, and it is my hair that has gone wannabe.

After obtaining my drink, I took a seat in the back, near the kitchen. The tattooed youngsters doing prep work in the kitchen had some sort of caustic (that's not a judgment, just a report) deathly-lawnmower heavy metal ripping from the speakers as they chopped scallions. These were pleasant, well-employed youth and I carried no animus, but I did nonetheless insert my ear buds and dial up a streaming music service that plays songs based on parameters toggled to reflect my personal preferences. About an hour in, I took a bathroom break and passed the open door of the kitchen where the chefs were now snapping their heads back and forth to the song "Lawyers, Guns and Money," by the late Warren Zevon. As this song was contemporaneous with my teenaged years, it did my 46-year-old heart good that the scallion-choppers found it acceptable and I returned to my seat feeling temporarily youthful.

Back to my computer, and back into the ear-buds. I was listening to the free version of the service, which meant it spun a few ads now and then, and I plugged in just in time to confront a question: If you are listening to a virtual radio station that generates its ads based on music you yourself have selected, what does it mean when you're 46 and trigger an insurance advert that starts out, "If you're a driver 50 and over...???"

I am beginning to feel withered and rancid, wrote the French philosopher Michel de Montaigne, and in that moment I knew why.

Five years have passed since I was fed that ad. Turns out it was but a warning shot. I have now crested my first half-century, and I am that driver. As a matter of fact I am that driver including the "and over." The last time I opened a YouTube video I was greeted with a banner warning me about "THE THREE WORST PROSTATE FOODS." The time before that the image was of a cranky oldster under the header, "I HATE SOCIAL SECURITY!" And then there was the one that said "THE ONE THING YOU SHOULD DO FOR YOUR PROSTATE EVERY MORNING." I'm a curious fellow, and no prude, but I just can't bring myself to click that last one, even if I do have a nursing license.

I now sit finishing this column in that same coffee shop. Over two decades I've been coming in here. I still like to pop in the ear buds and write. Time guarantees us nothing, but the day the algorithms serve up the first cremation or casket ad I'll go ahead and have that mocha because it will have been a pretty good run.

SNOT ROCKET

The column to follow includes both contemporary and 16th Century references to nasal secretions, so if that sort of subject matter curdles your reflective state, stop reading now. If, on the other hand, you like your history of philosophy mixed with third-grade level snickering, do proceed, and speaking of third grade, show me a better joke than, "You think it's mucus, but it's not!"

I once wrote a book that included an ode to the 'farmer snort,' a little trick for clearing the nasal passages that I'll leave mostly to your imagination except to say it involves laying one's finger aside of one's nose in the manner of St. Nick, but does not involve a handkerchief. My editor, a woman of class, distinction, and higher education, was put off by this paragraph, and suggested it be cut. Seated as she was in a nice Manhattan skyscraper, I couldn't blame her, but I—having that very morning conducted the maneuver to great satisfaction while feeding pigs—defended it on artistic principle. In the end the editor acquiesced but forbade me to use my alternate favorite term, "snot rocket."

Ever since Mrs. Amodt made us wear one pinned to our shirts in kindergarten, I have been creeped out by handkerchiefs. Linen, cotton, silk, whatever, it gurgled my guts to think it might be considered civilized to do what one does to a hankie—to put in it what one puts in it—and then carry it around for the rest of the day. That said, when one is raised in a state and situation in which a "snot rocket" is both acceptable behavior *and* high comedy, one sometimes doubts ones own cultural compass, and as such, I never went public with my handkerchief reservations, and instead tried to engage in intermittent cultural self-improvement beyond how best to blow my nose.

In the course of this latter I took to reading the essays of the French essayist and philosopher Michel de Montaigne. You will imagine my delight then, when—while reading philosophy on my smart phone in a deer stand—I came across this passage:

A French gentleman was always wont to blow his nose with his fingers (a thing very much against our fashion), and he justifying himself for so doing, and he was a man famous for pleasant repartees, he asked me, what privilege this filthy excrement had, that we must carry about us a fine handkerchief to receive it, and, which was more, afterwards to lap it carefully up, and carry it all day about in our pockets, which, he said, could not but be much more nauseous and offensive, than to see it thrown away, as we did all other evacuations. I found that what he said was not altogether without reason.

Vindication is all the sweeter when it arrives nicely aged via the late 1500s. I badly wanted to copy and paste the passage into an email and fire it off to my editor in New York, but chose not to disturb her as she is currently awaiting an overdue book manuscript, to which I will return as soon as I submit this column. That said, when the subject is next raised, I will brook no condescension, having been all this time comporting myself in the manner of a French gentleman.

POST-ELECTION LEAVES

Wrote this after the presidential election of 2016.

We got the leaves raked. Most of them, anyway. The thickest patches. Gathered and dropped them like blown insulation on the raspberry beds, the garlic beds, the asparagus beds. Dragged bushel after bushel across the yard on an old blue tarp and swooped them into a gigantic pile behind the woodshed. Next spring we'll redistribute them as needed, use them to mulch the garden, keep the weeds down around the deck and behind the hostas. One way or another they're headed back to the earth from whence they came.

At one point the whole family was in the yard, and it was nice to hear the wordless sound of it, the swish, swish, the brush and rustle of everyone working together. Between the four of us we wore out at least three rakes including one that has lost so many tines it looks like the skinny scarecrow cousin of the last decrepit Jack-O-Lantern. When we were done we stored the rakes in the shed, but we did have an impromptu discussion about whether or not rakes go on sale after Halloween just like all the candy and costumes. We'll keep an eye on the fliers.

It's been warmish and some of the garlic has sprouted, but we added another layer of those leaves to protect them when the white stuff finally does come, and there is no reason to expect they won't survive the winter. The chickens are a more likely threat, known as they have been to jump the run and scratch away all the mulch and cover, leaving a scatter of naked garlic bulbs lying all about like golf balls at the far end of a driving range. To that end we unrolled orange plastic fencing and tacked it down flat over the final application of leaves. In short we tucked that garlic in beneath an organic blankie then topped it off with a poultry-proof coverlet.

Then there were a few miscellaneous things. Move the deck furniture to the pole barn. Drain, roll and stow the garden hoses. Gather up miscellaneous windblown feed sacks. Chuck that old wooden gate on the burn pile. Finally everyone drifted off to their own thing until supper time.

It's odd to write this column knowing it won't publish until after an election that has the nation in tumult. Who knows what the state of things will be when you read it. I feel like I'm throwing an armful of leaves to the wind, not knowing which way they will blow, and possibly right back in my face. But I have addressed that elsewhere and in some cases the best we can do is tend our backyard and prepare for the season ahead.

PARK THEATER

Up in Hayward, Wisconsin, home of the Fresh Water Hall of Fame & Museum with its 143-foot long fiberglass musky (in whose maw some have recited their marriage vows surrounded by its hedge of knee-high teeth) there is an old movie house called the Park Theater that has been converted to a cozy venue with a stage for live shows. Last week some friends and I met up there to play music together.

We unloaded our gear in the usual glamorous fashion, lugging it through the back door beside the big blue dumpster. Setup was a breeze, as the theater includes a pair of volunteer sound techs who are very good at their jobs and had everything from monitors to microphones all set up for us. At many of our gigs we have to arrange all that stuff ourselves, and we are our own roadies. When your tour bus is the family minivan it is a rare luxury to simply roll in and plug in.

After sound check I stocked the merch table ("merch" is the universal road-dog term for "books, CDs, and t-shirts" which in turn can be translated to "gas money") in the lobby, which always smells of popcorn, even when no one is there.

Since set up and sound check had gone smoothly and efficiently and I wasn't under the gun time-wise, I enjoyed puttering around arranging the display and imagining how many thou-sands had filed through here over the years to buy a tub of buttery corn and a ticket for a show. The Park opened in 1948, and the marquee is a familiar sight at night along Hayward's main drag (does anyone still say "main drag?"). I will not lie it is nice to roll past it once and see your name in big plastic letters. Makes you want to do a good job.

The band and I have played the Park for many years now. It's one of those venues that feels like home away from home. Every time we return it seems the volunteer arts group has made another improvement. We have only one objection to the rehab of the building: There used to be a small dressing room in the back of the theater above the door of which was an illuminated sign reading "CRYING ROOM." Its original purpose was to give parents a soundproofed place to take a fussy baby so as not to disturb the other moviegoers, but we always thought it was perfectly labeled for a batch of delicate musicians and were sad when the sign disappeared.

The people came and we did our songs. From the stage you can just see their head-and-shoulder forms and the occasional flash of light off someone's glasses. In the end they applauded and asked us out for one more, which was a kindness. Then they left and we packed our gear and leftover merch back into our glamorous rides, and as we pulled away from the dumpster it was quiet in Hayward, the giant musky just up the road waiting for a mouthful of tourists.

GAME CAMERA

Down in the valley on the fencepost we have a game camera I hang in autumn in order to gather photographs of the big buck deer I won't get.

Game cameras have come a long way since our neighbor Ike put his first up over a pile of bear bait. In those days you set and pointed the camera in hope, went home, returned in a few days to pull the film, and then ran it up to the mall in Rice Lake where they had one of those stores that could develop your pictures in a mind-boggling one hour if you were willing to spring for the premium. Then—after, perhaps, grabbing an Orange Julius and swinging by Farm & Fleet—came the excitement of opening the packet of prints to see what sort of exotic wildlife had been captured up close and personal.

In the case of Ike, what you had was a whole lotta shots of a farmer in overalls making a pile of doughnuts.

Nowadays the camera captures ten-second videos of whatever passes before it, and the images are available as quickly as they can be downloaded. What we have here is the continuing encroachment of instant gratification. There's a lot of that going around.

On our cameras we get mostly videos of does and fawns meandering about. In the photos taken after dark, everything is rendered in gray and stark white, but the daytime images are richly colored. When no one is looking the deer nibble and nuzzle each other, prance like spring lambs, and oftentimes you see Ma looking back over her shoulder peevishly waiting for the youngsters to catch up. This week in a series of videos the big doe came through the viewfinder in business-like fashion, then the next several shots were of black deer noses blobbing in and out of frame as the fawns took turns sniffing the camera which clearly smelled of human goofball.

Last year a small buck noodled around in front of the camera for some time then turned away, presented his hindquarters, raised his tail, and did his very most basic business. By accident and as alternative to cartoons I happened to share these moving pictures with my grade-school daughter and nephews and there was much giggling, hooting and rolling around on the floor, although really nothing compared to the hilarious madness that ensued when I figured out you could run the footage in reverse. Somehow I never win any parenting awards.

Yesterday the images did include a crystal-clear close-up of a gorgeous buck with a remarkable set of antlers, all tall in the tine and big in the beam, although perhaps a tad narrow for your purists, of which I am not one. He was dipping his head and fidgeting as he stared into the lens, having—like the does before—caught a whiff of apex predator wafting off the mysterious camouflaged cycloptic box before him.

On my game cameras, the final vignette of each download always features a gray-whiskered human shuffling flat-footed down the trail and right up to the lens, the very final frozen image being a medically intimate view up twin nostrils, the shot you get when your apex predator is wearing bifocals.

DOG SHOW

Having fulfilled my duties as venison provider earlier in the week I was free to watch The National Dog Show with my nine-year old daughter before we headed north to the family farm for Thanksgiving. The youngster in question is a self-professed cat preferrer (to quote her at the age of six, unbidden, "I am a crazy cat lady") but as she bounced on the couch during the early stages of the canine pageant she also declared that "people" misunderstand her love for cats as a dislike of dogs.

At the risk of alienating portions of the readership I must reveal that my pet preference is exactly the reverse of hers. I grew up with farm dogs and cherished their reliable low-maintenance presence. Some were from the animal shelter, some were strays, all were mongrels. Some were smarter than others, some could do tricks, some could not, and fewer of them than you might suspect could fetch, but they were always a part of the surroundings. My brother taught one of them to climb the haymow ladder.

Having watched the mockumentary *Best In Show* many

multiple times more than I've watched the National and Westminster dog shows combined, it was a struggle to maintain the proper respectful frame of mind during the real thing. I kept hearing Fred Willard voiceovers in my head as opposed to the real commentators on TV. I had to resist the urge to shout favorite snippets. And whenever I saw the placid faces of the human handlers I imagined high-decibel tear-streaked dramas backstage.

But we stoked the woodstove, settled in, and enjoyed the proceedings. Early on, my daughter was looking forward to two categories: The Toy Group, and Best in Show. I read up on the Toy Group and was interested to see that their desirable qualities include "portability," which never occurred to us on the farm as we always had pickup truck beds and hay racks which render all dogs portable, and your finer mutts could vault aboard over a closed tailgate. I'm not so roughneck that I'll deny the dogs in the Toy Group are cute as heck, and I love to watch them run the arena, their legs doing the whole squirrel-in-a-hurry trippety-trap gait as if their Fast Forward button was perpetually stuck, but mostly it seems their greatest use would be dusting under the bed.

One by one we proceeded through the seven groups. Despite all the narration, I have no clue how the judges winnow the pack, and was utterly helpless in my predictions. My daughter squealed with delight at the final selection in the Toy Group based on the simple criterion that it was "so adorable." I wouldn't disagree except to say so were they all, and I stand by my claim that they are bred to hunt dust bunnies.

The Toy Group winner did not triumph as Best In Show and my cat-loving companion expressed disappointment in the winner (a greyhound, it looked like to me, at least I thought I recognized it from the side of the bus) but made it clear she held no animus, just an abundance of love for the tiniest dog of the bunch which it just now occurs to me could be used to polish its own trophy.

WINTER MAYBE

Down by the shed three plastic sleds rest on the last of the grass. They are inorganically bright blue, orange and purple against the earth. Easter colors on the last day of November. A saucer has caught some rain and a cat is at it, lapping.

For a single day last week there was just enough snow for the kids to sling snowballs, roll up a miniature snowman, and slide the slope out on the far side of the yard. It's a brief run. You have to shoot between two spruces and lean left so you don't hit the pole barn, but then there's a nice flat deceleration stretch before the pig fence. I watched from my room above the garage as the children cycled through, bundled and laughing and hooting and hollering and after each happy crash lying flat aback to smile at the sky.

Now the snow is gone and the skies are overcast. The kids are in school, the world turns, it is quiet here.

We know so much these days. Or at least we see and hear so much. *Knowing*, that's another thing. Some days it feels like everything offered is a deception. Lately I awaken at night hoping there are people smarter than I working on the important projects. I can write a line for a chuckle, I can write a line from the heart, but I have proven pretty powerless to do much more than provide word diversions. I'm not much at mending fences or bridging gaps. I'm sure not good at being loud.

I believe uncertainty is good for me. It is a source of humility. A catalyst for introspection. I recently spent the better part of a week in the woods. This is always a bracing stretch, as much scour as solace. The general resolution upon emergence was that I better rethink everything. The secondary resolution, having had a week to chew it over, is that one must not get needlessly dramatic and forget to keep doing the things one *is* good at. Even if we are polishing a tiny stone, it fits the foundation.

Winter hasn't even gotten it together to arrive, and already I'm tired of darkness. Already I'm pulling for solstice, just so we can rotate toward light. But as my parents told me and as I have told my children, you can't just go around tripping on your lip. There is work to be done. I must fix a smile in the face of the grayness, drag those colorful sleds to the top of the hill, put them in position for when the next snow falls.

Whoops, nope. That's metaphorical mush designed to make me feel better while solving nothing. Rather—in defense of normalcy and a brighter future and the needs of civilized society as a whole—I shall catch the residing child in question on her trip in from the school bus and instruct her to put those sleds back in the shed where they belong. Also, fill the cat's water dish. We must press on.

PUSHUPS

I have been doing a lot of pushups lately, which is to say a few more than none. This is not a New Year's resolution situation as I embarked upon this regimen the week before Christmas, and have only taken four or five days off since. It is important that I not overwork my elbow and shoulder joints. Also, I don't want to have to go out and buy a whole bunch of new shirts with bigger armholes.

By way of goal-setting I recently studied a photograph of former NFL tight end Shannon Sharpe (brother of Sterling, who, if he hadn't suffered a neck injury, might have teamed up with Brett Favre to bring three or four more Lombardi trophies home to the Dairy State) in which Shannon's triceps appear to have been composed of extruded marble, boa constrictor DNA, and dragline cables. It is difficult to compare my triceps to Shannon Sharpe's triceps because when that picture was taken Shannon's body fat was running just a celery string above five percent, whereas mine is currently that plus a dozen doughnuts and a layer of fry bread.

On the subject of professional football player triceps,

chance and self-employment once took me to a stadium tunnel just prior to the player introductions before a Tennessee Titans versus Pittsburgh Steelers football game. Someone eased up beside me and I turned only to find my nose half an inch from a hairy tree trunk, which in fact turned out to be an upper arm. The triceps in this case was not so Shannon Sharpe-ly cut, but the circumference and texture of the limb as a whole was that of a slimmish warthog. I raised my gaze, up, and up, and up, and eventually saw the face of Bruce Matthews, now a retired Hall of Fame offensive lineman and uncle of Clay Matthews the Third, currently playing for the Green Bay Packers and whom I once observed in a photo (taped on the wall in the backroom of a local coffee shop where the waitresses gather) doing pushups while draped in chains and his own flowing locks.

I intend to work up to the chains slowly, beginning perhaps with a small bracelet. The flowing locks will have to wait until the follicular pharmaceuticals improve.

But for now, no chains, no juicing, just pushups. The simplest sort of exercise. I have a little buzzer on my watch that reminds me throughout the day, at which point I drop and rap out five, sometimes seven, in a row, without stopping. Unless I get an electric shock sensation running down my right arm, in which case I reposition. Or stop and treat the pain with a doughnut.

Deep into the second week of this physical fitness spree I feel myself firming up and typing with much greater power. I will pace myself so as not to crack the keyboard or blow up so quickly that steroids be suspected, but check with me next year when I will wrap myself in golden chains and arm-wrestle Clay Matthews and his golden ponytail. May the best man...go easy on me.

SKIING

I stood atop my skis at the crest of the Black Diamond slope, squinting like Hans Klammer. If you remember Hans Klammer you are old like me, because he won the gold medal for downhill skiing in the 1976 Winter Olympics, and as Wikipedia later told me, his name is Franz, not Hans, but such are the mists of time, and I figure after all these years that's a decent A-minus. The squinting was less about manfully surveying the snowscape than it was about me trying to remember.

Ol' Franz could really smoke the slopes, and when I was young and skiing the mighty hummocks of Christie Mountain near Bruce, Wisconsin, or Rice Lake's now-defunct Hardscrabble, I used to bend my knees and tuck my poles the way I had seen Franz do in *Sport* magazine and go *schuss* (a straight downhill run at high speed) top-to-bottom in with tears freezing out the side of my eyes, leaving a trail of Brut aftershave in my wake, and secretly hoping that girl on the chairlift was checking my style. In fact I skied like a farm kid famous within the family mainly for running into things, and part of the reason I Klammer'd every hill was because I never quite mastered that effortlessly lovely back-and-forth weave some folks can do like their legs are soldered together at the ankles. My ankles were always at least a yard apart and sometimes on opposite sides of a birch tree.

And so it was better to just point for the chalet and let'er rip.

These days my let'er rip days are tempered by a breathtaking health insurance deductible, one floppy leg, downward-trending testosterone levels, and the fact that I go downhill skiing about once every seven years. And so, having traveled to Bruce Mound Winter Sports Area just outside Merillan, Wisconsin, with my family for a day of winter's fun, I squinted down that black diamond run once more and cut across to the blue square run, which I descended with cautious carving, in a crouched stance reminiscent less of Franz Klammer than a hipshot farmer trying to corner a pig on a frozen pond with his feet duct-taped to a pair of warped two-by-fours.

My teenaged daughter joined me for several runs. She was astride a snowboard, and thus looked cooler than I just standing still, something as an "older" parent I can tell you teens do all the time. After a few rounds with her I diverted to what we used to call "the bunny hill," where my wife was helping our youngest child learn to ski. There was a lot of falling and failing, and then finally, that one trip where it all clicked, and the child completed the entire run upright.

To celebrate, all four of us ended the day over on the tubing run. You flop on top of the tube and ride it down the giant trough. Simple. Speedy. *Schuss* for the rest of us. You hear a lot more laughter amongst the inner tubes than on the black diamond runs. And you can just wave your ankles any which way.

BYE-BYE BEARDIE

My big beard is gone.

I've never been a big beard guy in any sense of the adjective. Stubble, sure, and pretty frequently, because shaving bores me, and of course there is the annual deer hunting beard, grown around here mostly by instinct, but I've never sustained one to the point where you'd assign me my own trapline.

This year I've done it twice. The first one just kinda snuck up on me last summer. It began through standard razor neglect. Then, when it achieved sufficient mass to interfere with eating spaghetti, I decided it was time it went, and said so. Overhearing this, my younger daughter pled with me to keep growing it out big like her uncle (my brother, whose beard has been pioneer-like for decades) so she could see what it looked like.

I like to please my children, but I don't *live* to please my children; that said, she was so earnest in her pleas I figured I'd let it grow a while longer. By July it looked like something you might find while *checking* your trapline. In August someone sent me a photo taken at a public event in which I was speaking while brightly backlit and it appeared my face was afloat in a nimbus of electrified cotton.

Shortly thereafter I appeared in a play and had to cut it off.

Then came autumn, and the deer hunting beard. And then, after deer hunting, a renewed plea from the young one that I let it grow out again, this time, "So I can trim it." Having reached December and with subzero temperatures inbound I consented.

My two favorite things about my beard are 1) the way it camouflages my deteriorating jawline, and 2) how it keeps my face warm during below-zero chicken chores or other outdoor pursuits including sledding, skiing, and scraping snow off the photovoltaic panels on the granary roof (please install more photovoltaic panels—ours have been great—but don't install them on your granary roof). So it was easy to keep it growing right through into January, although the food thing really does become an issue: How is one to maintain the illusion of being a rough-and-tumble bearded back-woodser when the foam from his Holiday Spice latte is right there on his mustache, overhanging the quiche crumbs snagged on the chin overgrowth below?

So last night I sat on a stool before the bathroom mirror, handed the younger daughter a scissors and electric clippers, and turned her loose. The session lasted over an hour. There were a lot of laughs, some pain, but no blood. The beard underwent several permutations, the penultimate manifestation being a mustache I hadn't worn since 1984. After she snipped that away, I shaved my face clean. "Welcome back," said my wife, who is not into whiskers.

I swept the beard up then, carried it outside in a dustpan, and shook it to the winter wind, which at that moment was blowing negative double chill-digits, icily tweaking my naked cheeks as it whispered, *big mistake, Buster.*

SNOWED IN

The snow fell heavily while I was in town running errands but I was still surprised to discover how bad the roads were when I headed home midafternoon. After a lifetime of navigating Wisconsin blizzards with two-wheel drives, my wife and I recently bought our first all-wheel-drive vehicle (she handled the haggling and Craigslist sifting, I tagged along to sign the paperwork), but even with that extra assist things got tenuous and sideways down there on that stretch off the big hill where it always drifts over first.

The next test came at the dead end road leading to our driveway. The road is built at a precipitous pitch, and for years what you did under snowy conditions was take a half-mile run at it and just go like mad. "Pour the cobs to'er," as we used to say. Then our erstwhile local highway commissioner "improved" the intersection, putting a kink in it so the straight shot was no longer an option and the odds of making the hilltop in a two-wheel drive pretty much vanished beneath the first three snowflakes. The new all-wheeler chewed straight up and past the mailbox without trouble.

Our elder daughter (in her first winter with a driver's license) had early-morning band practice and had driven the family van to school. The younger was riding the school bus home. I excavated the plow truck and met the elder daughter in town so she could get valuable experience driving the van in the slush-rut mess but not wind up stranded. She made it home fine. I plowed the driveway while my wife and elder daughter began shoveling sidewalks and a path to the garage. Then I met the school bus at the base of the hill to pick up the young one and spare the driver the excitement of a failed ascent.

The younger one and I took over the snow management duties—shoveling the deck and path out to the chicken coop, clearing the photovoltaic panels on the granary roof for the second time in as many days (I let the 9 year-old off the hook on that last one)—and other outside evening chore duties while my wife went in to begin supper preparations and the teenager fetched a load of firewood. It was well dark by the time I attached the pan heater to the plow truck. When the younger one and I got into the house there were biscuits to be mixed, and she leapt to it.

The kitchen table was covered with homework and mail, and the kitchen chairs hung with drying snow gear, so we ate supper on a folding card table in the living room near the woodstove, talking about a trip we might like to take next summer and reviewing the recent season's accumulated Christmas cards. We are like any family; things are not always harmonious. We are a stubborn and determined bunch, some of us quietly so, others emphatically so. There is your standard sibling pick-picking, a snappish word here and there, the occasional storm-off. But by and large we get along, and this was one of those good nights, when the snow unexpectedly pushed us into a different schedule, pushed us into extra work, and pushed us into a different space, made all the warmer by the closeness of our knees beneath the tiny table as outside the snow settled into silent night.

IDIOT DRIVER

Earlier today some idiot—and I deploy the word with neither reservation nor qualification nor apology—decided to pass a line of oncoming cars at a speed far in excess of the posted 55 mph limit and criminally short of a safe distance. I know this because I occupied the lane into which the idiot pulled. When he careened back into the flow of traffic, I rose up in my seat in order to shoot eyeball death rays through his windshield but I was immediately distracted by another idiot —let's just call him Idiot in Triplicate—who whipped out into my line of travel to make a pass of his own and was inbound on my air bag at a crazed rate of speed which I calculated based on the rapid expanding ratio of his grill to my windshield and the fact that his raggedy minivan was spewing black smoke as he stomped the foot-feed. As he dove back over the centerline I could without exaggeration see the whites of his eyes, which were a nice match to the shade of my knuckles. Our door handles flashed within feet of each other.

This was not bad driving, this was malevolent stupidity. In the mirror I could see another vehicle forced to the shoulder by the Idiot in Triplicate, and for a split-second I entertained the fantasy of whippin' a U-ey and getting myself into real trouble, but reality and more oncoming traffic overrode the option, and I had to settle for fuming and quaking.

The fuming was on my own behalf. The quaking was not. The quaking was because my first thought was of my daughter, in her first year of driving. So far so good, nothing taken for granted. But every time she steps out of the door with the keys in her hand, I tell her one of two things, and neither of them is "Drive safely!" I've never understood that one, or the other common version, "Drive careful!" Seems that oughta be a given. Kinda like saying, "Breathe always!" Instead, I either say, "Go with care," or "Watch out for the other guy."

I choose the first phrase because she has reached that level of callow proficiency where it is easy to assume one has seen and navigated it all. The level where young drivers begin to slough off many of the rules and habits inculcated by the driver's ed instructor (the same rules and habits that only months ago the young driver loved to invoke from the passenger seat in admonishment of the motoring parent). It is in this first flush of ease that the sudden sad surprises come. "Go with care" is my attempt at a gentle reminder: *you are still new at this; you are transporting precious cargo.*

"Watch out for the other guy," is obvious in light of today's opening paragraph. Since the day she got behind the wheel I have told her to drive anticipating that every approaching vehicle is about to cross the centerline. Today at first opportunity, I told her the story. So she would know it's not just her paranoid old man making stuff up. Later she put her younger sister in the car and they headed into town for lessons of some sort. I told her what I tell you: Go with care. Watch out for the other guy. And that second other guy.

CARIBBEAN WORK DAY

We had the opportunity to visit relatives in a sunny place and did so. In 48 hours we went from shoveling snow to digging sand from our shorts. At the moment it seems anything I write—especially describing experiences of extreme privilege such as this, and I acknowledge it as such—must be filtered through a scrim of humility in the face of current events. But I am also trying to live beyond my generation and continue to hope that by drawing my children into environs where people different than we have their own ways of being neighborly the kids will grow up less willing to navigate based on misallocations of fear. Lest you think this is some sort of self-congratulatory after-school special, we also spent time during this getaway arguing about screen time, chores, bedtime, and general scheduling. There was some huffing and grumping and retreating to rooms, and that's just speaking for myself.

Within hours of our arrival we spent some time in and on the Caribbean, and there is no better way for a well-larded cheesehead fresh out of the slush to realize he is such than to stand shin-deep in the surf as the sun converts his scalp into a crepe skillet. The addition of a neon pink snorkel mask and flippers heighten the effect. To see me "hit the surf" is to observe an albino walrus with balance issues trying to exit the tavern only to belly-flop into the stock tank. When I finally wind up floating face down, I am amazed to see fish that have clearly escaped from someone's aquarium. When you are raised on walleye and northern, you go ga-ga over the simplest tropical minnow.

Another benefit of unseasonable (to me) sun (let's also call it "cheater's sun") is that when you spend half the day lurching around in foot fins and sweating like you're baling hay when you're just sitting there, your brain rewires itself so that eating feels like an essential and hard-earned ritual necessary to keep up with all the calories that evaporate simply through nonstop exposure to sun. The writer Jim Harrison once wrote that "Only in the Midwest is overeating considered an act of heroism," and he was right, but the sad subtopic is that when we overeat during the cramped dark days of winter the post-Calvinist guilt kicks in. Empty calories are a self-defeating bulwark against the encroaching ice banks in your brain, whereas down here with your head addled by the scent of 50 SPF sunblock, you rediscover food as a form of celebration compatible with the environs.

At one point during the vacation we took a day to help our relatives do some projects: painting, cleaning and fixing windows, general maintenance. Considering the free room and board we were receiving, this little break from the sunburn schedule seemed the least we could do. There was grumbling from junior quarters, to which I responded, "Hey, how 'bout you go out and drag the tarp off the woodpile and haul in about three loads?" at which point washing the screens suddenly seemed like a form of celebration compatible with the environs.

HOME FROM THE BEACH

This one originates from 36,000.7 feet above sea level. The decimal-point specificity comes courtesy of a digital touch screen embedded in the seatback before me. The display additionally informs me that we are due into Minneapolis two hours and one minute from now, with touch-down predicted for 10:36 p.m.

Also in rotation is this bracing bit of data: just feet from our seats, outside the skin of the aircraft, it is 72 degrees below zero. I have directed the attention of my two traveling companions (daughters aged 9 and 17) toward this information in the hope that it may somehow mitigate the fact that we are returning to Wisconsin in January after ten days spent visiting their grandparents in a place where the thermometer basically locks in at 80, the sun crosses the sky in slow scorch mode, and the sand in your toes is from the beach—as opposed to that old trash can in the garage where you mix it with rock salt in a bean can before spreading it on the driveway so the meter reader doesn't wind up in lawyers and traction.

We know what weather awaits. These days we can stand

amidst the palm trees with our cellphones and get a weather report from the very coordinates of the barnyard. Via Wi-Fi and security cam we can inspect the state of the snow banks while geckos dart around poolside. As the surf laps our sunburned thighs we can dial up the local TV news app and watch our hometown weather person deliver a forecast that translates to, "Um, I'd stay right where you are."

But: School. School, and work. And friends and neighbors willing to do the cat and chicken chores only so long. So home we go, into the snow.

It's just the three of us: Mom (also known as my wife, but once we had children my mom became grandma, and my wife became Mom) stayed behind for a few extra days with her mom. Both women saw us off at the airport, and the last we saw of our Mom was her peeking through a gap in the smoked glass of the security doors at customs, smiling that tight second-thoughts smile triggered perhaps by the idea of separation from her beloved daughters, perhaps by the idea of leaving them in care of the guy who gets lost on the way to the garage with the recycling.

We are sad to be without her, but happy to let her stay. She has earned this respite in a multitude of ways, to say nothing of years, and we hope she gets the rest and quiet she deserves. We feel off-kilter without her, of course. Even more so now that it is nighttime, just the three of us in a row, the jetliner darkened, lit softly by little islands of digital glow. We are tired, with another hour of flight, then two hours of driving in a slowly thawing van before—we hope—arriving home around 2 a.m., which will actually feel like 4 a.m. given the time zone we've been operating in. Come morning, I'll let the kids sleep in, give them time to rest their eyes before the big adjustment from sun on sea to sun on snow. The chickens will greet us like they'd greet anyone with a bucket of feed.

HOME SICK

We got home from our family trip on Friday morning. Saturday morning the water quit. Sunday morning we woke up sick. By "we" I mean my two daughters and me, as my wife had stayed for an extra few days with her relatives in the Caribbean.

It was 4:30 a.m. when the bathroom faucet spit, coughed, and went dry. Naturally I went back to bed, theory being you give the plumbing some time alone to sort itself out and by sunrise all is well. This often works with old pickup trucks. Sadly, by light of day, nothing had changed. Not so much as a hiss or drip. I conducted a ceremonial routine of trying several different faucets, throwing breakers, and directing all the power of my third eye at the switchbox that controls the well. Then, based on a vague recollection of a conversation I'd had with our plumber in the past, I watched three YouTube videos on how to reset the pressure tank, lugged an air tank into the basement, spritzed some air around, and then, upon opening a few valves only to find everything bone dry, decided it was time to call for professional help. In fact, the time for that was the minute the faucet failed, but I am dedicated, determined, and thick in the head.

After a few calls and some smartphone photographs (our basement is a muddy dungeon plumbed contemporaneous with the first Grover Cleveland administration and is done no favors by flash photography) it was determined that the well pump may have failed. The crew with the truck was available, but it being a weekend, it would cost an extra $50 an hour. I set an appointment for Monday.

Meanwhile, it was sanatorium city, the three of us hacking and holding our heads and trudging around through drifts of crumpled Kleenex, the dirty dishes accumulating in teetering stacks that reminded me of bachelorhood. A friend of mine down the road was away, so I snuck the kids in to use his shower once and get some potable water, but other than that we asked no quarter. I even taught my daughters to flush the toilet using melted snow. One day their children will tire of hearing this.

Come Monday we were still sick and I kept the kids home from school. The well repairmen showed up early. One man studied the well cap and said something along the lines of, "Yah, y'don't see many of those anymore." He then referenced the need for a boom truck, 150 feet of cable, tens of thousands of pounds of extractive pressure, and the possibility that the number on the check might require a comma. "But first, let's verify that it's not something more simple," he said. Shortly thereafter he emerged from the basement. The problem was in an electrical switch. In under an hour it was fixed, the water came pouring forth, and we were still sick, but showered and the dishwasher was purring. Some of your truest heroes arrive armed with a voltage tester.

By Wednesday we were still prone to coughing fits but improving. My wife returned the same day with sea breeze in her hair. "I'm sorry you had to go through all that," she said, after I briefed her. I affected a selfless shrug, but then, having spent perhaps a third of our marriage on the road, leaving her to handle everything and worse, said the only thing I could: We both got exactly what we deserved.

HIGH FASHION

I have just been to a fashion show in my own house, featuring me. The runway was the hallway to the bathroom, with a dogleg left past the woodstove into the living room. The audience sat on the couch and consisted of my wife and two daughters. Flash photography was forbidden, as Dad does not wish to wind up shirtless on Snapchat in light of certain lard-based gravitational issues.

My sartorial state is a source of long-term despair for everyone in my immediate family except for immediately me. There was a time now decades distant when I cared how I dressed, and this led to some egregious overshoots including bolo clips, popped collars, a pink silk head scarf, wrestling shoes worn with my jeans tucked in, open blazers with the cuffs rolled, more than one trench coat, and, for a while, an affectation of hats. The arc of fashion bends toward reality, and eventually I settled into a reliable groove of sturdy boots, no-name jeans, and free t-shirts. This has saved me a lot of time, cash, and retrospective humiliation.

As a clothes rack, my body is a stack of used tires. Even fit and fine I've always been shortish and stocky-ish, and no matter what those men's magazine photo spreads tell you, nothing dresses a man better than being six feet tall with narrow hips and just one chin. Unfortunately, recently my wife read one of those men's magazines, specifically a section on how to decorate certain body types ("balding husky," anyone?) and, after a trip to town centered mainly on clearance bins, the three people I share my house and life with staged an intervention.

Apparently the triggering event was a recent speaking event at which I appeared in my favorite pair of jeans, which are still my favorite even though I have waddled a hole through the left inner thigh. There was concern that from an audience perspective it might be possible to determine my underwear preference. It was also noted that the t-shirt I was wearing bore evidence of the grease from a pre-millennial gas station mozzarella stick. Sometimes I think they're just looking for things to criticize.

I had packed the van for a concert that evening and run into the house for a quick shower when I found the three of them waiting on the couch beside a card table stacked with clothing. There was no escape, and so it began: Into the bathroom to change, then out in my socks to stump through the gauntlet of gaze: My wife, looking on benevolently, hoping for the best; my 9-year old, mostly giggling; and my 17-year old, mostly horrified. There were folded arms, pursed lips, and once, when I made the mistake of parading through shirtless in a pair of decidedly undersized "skinny" jeans, outright hoots. Turns out, these particular trousers caused an anatomical displacement I am told is called a "muffin-top."

But if merciless assessment is love, I am beloved. Eventually the jury approved one pair of pants, three t-shirts that didn't advertise anything, and a button shirt that goes with my eyes while simultaneously minimizing the muffin top. That night when I took the stage I felt confident and grateful and then on the long drive home after midnight that t-shirt collected a drop of gas station hot dog grease and now it really suits me.

TRUCK SNACKS

I have a very bad habit of eating late at night. It may be my undoing. It certainly put me in a bind last week, when instead of driving straight home from a job in a nearby town just 20 minutes from the farm where our refrigerator is filled with fresh and original victuals, I pulled into a gas station in order to buy some food, "food" in this case being a euphemism for "snacky treats not available at home where things run heavy to fiber, crisp veggies, and the occasional kale-based smoothie." As I shut off our old plow truck and slunk into the convenience store, my internal voice was saying, "You are making naughty nutritional decisions and possibly violating your marriage vows." But then this other internal voice hollered, "Hey! Day-old apple fritters! Only a buck!"

It is not important to tell you what I bought, although somewhere there exists security cam footage of me chasing the last dill pickle slice around the vat with a plastic spoon so that in a pinch I could say I ate something green with my roller dog. I hustled back to the truck with my contraband

and turned the key. The starter cranked and cranked but nothing else happened.

My face went as white as a powdered mini-donut. It wasn't because of the truck. It dies about every four months. But how was I gonna explain *where* and *when* it died? Nervously, I nibbled at a kettle chip. Then I called for a tow, but for reasons having to do with the attached snow plow, none was available until morning.

Now I had two additional problems. One was: How to get home. The second was how to explain to my wife why I was at the gas station after midnight. I briefly considered saying I was getting gas, but A) I had just filled the truck the day prior and she knew it, and B) the truck died in the parking stall nearest the store entrance, nowhere near a pump. Even if I went with the refueling ruse, I'd still have to explain why I re-parked the truck so near the doughnuts.

Desperate, I got a can of starting fluid and in a contortion worthy of a roughneck acrobat, pumped the accelerator and twisted the starter while reaching around with my free hand to spray bottle throttle in the general direction of the carburetor. The engine fired and rattled like a diesel, but wouldn't sustain. I briefly considered driving home with the hood up while spritzing the engine compartment with ether, but suspected this would lead to arrest and cracked pistons.

It was now nearly 1 a.m. Rather than wake my wife, I arranged a ride home, and slipped quietly into bed. At dawn, I told her the darn truck had died again. "Where is it?" she asked. I told her, and her mouth said, "Okay." What her eyes said was a little more complicated. You could tell she was doing a little logistical math based on prior knowledge of my bad habits.

I told her the truth. I would like to claim this as testament to my character, but I had done some math of my own. This was clearly one of those situations where the first cut is the deepest, but at least you don't wind up tangled in the razor wire. Furthermore, she can detect the scent of artificial cheese dust from forty paces. I was rewarded for my honesty when, upon returning to the scene of the crime, the truck started at the first touch, saving me the price of a tow. I drove directly to the repair shop, arriving greatly fortified by a two-day-old apple fritter I found in a bag down by the gear shift.

TAPPING MAPLES

It was the third week of February when Jan and Gale tapped our maples. This was mighty early, but when the sap runs, you bring the buckets.

Jan and Gale are our neighbors in the regional, if not next-door, sense, and they have a route they run with their Subaru and trailer, gathering sap from various locations including four maples in our yard. It's a delicious exchange for us. We simply have to keep an eye on the pails and decant them into a larger container as needed. In return, we receive a percentage of the syrup yielded after boiling. Gale is very businesslike about the whole operation, tracking each site's production on a spreadsheet so that each family gets its fair share.

Of our four tapped trees, two are gigantic and yield steadily. Of the two smaller, the one in front of the garage is tentative and unreliable, while the one up by my office has been flowing more freely every year, and has grown to a diameter that will now support two taps.

In the first 24 hours our trees ran moderately well, but then the temperature cycle broke and the dripping stopped.

This week, however, we got a couple of the just-below-freezing nights and warm days needed to prime the pump again, and soon we were well on our way to the first 40 gallons of sap required to make one gallon of syrup.

One day things ran so well that when I stepped out of my office I heard a steady *splat-splat* and realized the bucket was full and the overflow was dripping into the mud. It took me maybe two minutes to run to the house for a funnel, pour the sap into the main container, and rehang it, but it felt far longer with that little metronome of lost sweetness running in the background the whole time, each *splat* a glistening sugar-drop that would never see the top of a pancake. As I rehung the pail a, crystal clear bead of sap emerged from a scar in the bark at eye level. Naturally I leaned in and touched it with the tip of my tongue, the capillary effect drawing it coolly across those taste buds tuned to sweet.

I have taught both my daughters to do the same, and in one of those moments that jolt your spirit, I recalled the first time Jan and Gale came with their taps, and how my elder daughter loved to run around checking the buckets with me. She was seven then. It was our first year on the farm, and I have a photo of her lifting the lid to peek into one of the pails, her little nose just clearing the lip. Back then the two-tap office maple wouldn't even support a single spout. Now it's as thick as me and the little girl is seventeen and six feet tall.

It's a good thing for my children that someone else does our "sugaring," as it is one of those things old Dad would likely have never gotten off his "some day" list. This morning I mumbled through the kitchen on my way to the office as the girls were eating breakfast before school, each of them finishing a pancake drizzled with maple syrup, the provenance of which they understood to be natural and nearby— and therein lies my deepest gratitude to Jan and Gale, upon whom I wish a blessed run of freeze and thaw.

FORGET IT

If absent-mindedness were an Olympic event I would be on ALL the Wheaties boxes.

Today's evidence to that effect establishes itself in the fact that right now I am on an airplane typing this column on a tiny electronic device better suited to rotting the brain with digital games. Not that I'd be able to detect rotting of the brain based on this morning's episode, in which I left my backpack (containing four days' worth of essential work papers, my laptop, a parking pass required upon arrival, and a neck pillow I am right now missing very much) upon the kitchen floor.

I was an hour down the road with the airport nearly in view when I realized it was gone. My eyes flew open wide. Then I said something in possibly French which translated for church means, "I AM DISHEARTENED!"

I hold several world records for absent-mindedness. This being a brief column I'll just hit the highlights, which include: discovering up to three pair of reading glasses parked atop my head; a pathological inability to make coffee without wandering off—sometimes down to the pole barn, once to another country—between the filter and the grounds; a Dead Sea's worth of coffee spilled from cups placed "just for a second" on the car roof; two separate pre-dawn incidents in which I hiked to, climbed into, and secured myself to, deer stands only to discover that my deer rifle was trigger-locked, with the key some 80 acres distant; the same trigger lock scenario only it was goose hunting, it was a six-mile drive, and there were rude firefighter pals present who never let me forget it; and once (this is where we separate the wannabes from the professionals) starting out the driveway with one car, parking it to run back to fetch something I had told myself NOT TO FORGET, and then leaving in another car, only to find the driveway blocked by the first car, door ajar, engine idling.

I travel with and for work a lot. My backpack is my office. I sling it over my shoulder out of habit and hardly know how to walk without it. And yet somehow this morning I managed —in between loading the suitcases and feeding the chickens —to set off without it. I wasn't even running late. Perhaps that was the problem, as usually I tear around in a hypertensive sweat-fest, trying to throw everything together at the last minute. This results in me making a series of concentric loops, the upshot being, were I under the gun, I might have tripped over the backpack on the third pass. Efficiency is the enemy of...I forget.

This being the cloud-based age, I have been able, through the use of my phone and an antique electronic tablet, to obtain and reconstruct about half of what I need, and at the very least knock out this column. Meanwhile a neighbor has arranged to overnight the backpack to me at a hotel tomorrow morning, where it and I will be reunited in the lobby. I will sling it over my shoulder and head straight back up the elevator to my room to start working, and it won't be until I am standing at the door that I will realize my key card is locked in the room.

SAGUARO

This morning on the business news a man said we were due for "a tradeable correction of consequence." Recognizing a call for action when I hear one, I immediately reviewed our portfolio of firewood and chickens. Barring avian flu or weasels, it appears we will be able to fry eggs well into spring. Beyond that I'm in the same boat with the rest of you losers.

I recently returned from a gigantic book festival in Tucson, Arizona, where for two days it was possible to act as if snow plows and dead batteries didn't exist and informed, thoughtful discussions of literature outside the academy were commonplace. Lest I overdo it I should reveal that I used some of my microphone time to describe the remarkable physics generated by a sneezing cow. In short, we're talking organic rear-end ballistics, and as with any form of artillery, you would do well to seek cover. As for the old farmer who told me, "Cows don't sneeze, they cough," he is correct as bovines go, but in terms of humor he missed the point.

The bookish Tucson crowd was happy to be among books but there was a thread of tension running throughout that was not so subtly tied to the state of the nation, a nation hatched, after all, by those oft-cited Founding Fathers who, before wrapping themselves in the flag, wrapped themselves in literature and philosophy—both currently facing the future as a grape faces a steamroller.

Or so it can feel. But in the lovely cocoon of the festival we strode around with bound paper under our arms and in our tote bags (if you sewed together all the tote bags generated by book festivals, public radio, and the conference industry in general you could stitch up a sunbrella sufficient to reverse global warming) enjoying the idea that humans are tenacious in many different ways. The headlines were dominated by large font capital letters, but we were down in the footnotes, where you will still find strength and resolve and the seeds of new voices bound to sprout up and split foundations crumbling in part through main force but mostly the dead weight of presumption.

Despite claims of exceptionalism, there is a point—I am paraphrasing all the history books here—when every society bites itself in the butt. Time will tell if we are there, or if we can open our jaws wide enough, and what if it is so? Down there in the desert I welcomed the opportunity to diversify the portfolio of my head and heart with voices of all styles, tenor, and heritage, each of them essential to my future no matter the future.

Outside my Tucson hotel room door there stood a saguaro. If ever there was a simple way to remind a cheesehead that he is outside the state lines, a saguaro is it. This one —and millions of others nearby—stand because at some point it was decided the bulldozers should stop and the saguaros should stay. This was an artistic decision. The economic merits were debatable, but without question it produced a correction of consequence. So it is they still publish books; so it is we still read them.

FALLING FORWARD

In an ongoing attempt to prevent my body from transforming utterly into gas station doughnuts and beef sticks, whenever work takes me on the road, I try to maintain some sort of fitness regimen to combat the hours spent slouched behind the wheel, running (my mouth) in place, or lying flat on my back and scarfing vending machine candy bars while watching basic motel cable at 2 a.m.

In this instance "try to" and "sort of" are not just throwaway phrases. They are quite intentionally deployed to mitigate any misperception my use of the phrase "fitness regimen" might create, which is to say, sometimes a sock-footed shuffle up the hallway to get those candy bars is your peak aerobic moment of the day. Bless the person who inserted the word "target" in the phrase "target heart rate," for therein we were given wiggle room.

But. One must get serious or die. Recently I arose distended at dawn in a hotel room and put my foot in an empty pizza box. Talk about standing in shame. There was much deskwork to be done, but I firmly resolved to first load it into my backpack and hike to a distant coffee shop I had passed when arriving the night before. Using a popular online mapping site I located the shop and was pleased to see it would be a six-mile round trip, the very distance Abraham Lincoln walked to return three pennies he had overcharged a customer. In other words: an honorable distance. Although now that we dragged Abe into it I am compelled to admit it was 2.7 miles each way—I am rounding up in the interest of fitness.

I hiked over without incident. Got my work done. Set out on the return trip. The sun was bright, the sidewalks clear. I strode purposefully, in support of the idea that calories can be burned by intent. I was making good time and feeling lean when I caught my toe on a crack and was immediately launched into one of those high-speed forward-tilt scramblers where your feet desperately try to catch up with your forehead in the manner of a drunken triple-jumper. There was lurching and windmilling of the sort you might see were a walrus to catch a hind flipper coming out of the starting blocks. In my defense, that backpack impeded my inner ballerina.

There came a point when I realized I was not going to pull out of this nosedive. Faced with nothing but concrete at my face, I rotated into a last-ditch half-twist and embarked on an intentional ferocious headfirst full-body lunge into a snow bank. It was cold in there, and I didn't linger. I scrambled to my feet and hustled off covered head to toe in snow that clung to me like powdered sugar to a gas station doughnut. Just feet away, the boulevard was busy, and I have my pride, so like a batsman hit by a pitch, I didn't stop to check for blood until I got back to the hotel. Indeed there were raw spots, and holes in the elbow of my shirt and the knee of my pants. I found a cold piece of cheesy bread and ate it so my body would have the power to heal itself. While chewing I formulated a theory that fitness is dangerous. Then I thought of the busy boulevard and how even now some of those people were telling their families what they'd seen, and I thought, son, that was the most spectacular thing you've done all month. You are welcome, good commuters of Grafton.

POLE BARN

The battle of the pole barn is set to resume.

First of all, because sometimes I get emails: where I come from, a "pole barn" is a shed constructed of corrugated steel nailed to a framework of poles and rafters. We have two big ones. They were here when we bought the place, left over from when it was a fully operational dairy farm. One was intended to shelter large machinery; the other to store giant piles of shell corn.

Another pause for definition: While some will lobby for "shelled" corn out of a didactic sense of descriptive specificity, if you wish to blend in down at the feed mill, I guarantee you want to go with "shell" corn.

First thing that happened the moment I laid eyes on those pole barns a decade ago was I had a vision, and the vision was this: My old pickup truck, my mother-in-law's tractor, some miscellaneous mowing and tilling equipment, a smattering of lumber stacks, and my tools, all arranged as neatly as a museum display, with broad paths of access to and between everything.

Well, sure. Allow me to present a proposal having to do with universal physics: The junk-sucking vacuum created by an empty outbuilding is directly proportional—nay, *exponentially* proportional—to the size of that outbuilding and in fact may exert a pull equivalent to that of a black hole capable of causing the earth to collapse inward upon itself.

Now imagine you have two of those right out there in the yard.

About three years into our residence both pole barns were stacked, wedged and cluttered to the walls with all manner of treasure and detritus. After failing to locate the battery charger that winter, come warm weather I attacked the problem with broom, shovel, and shelving. Such a deep, contented sigh I let go as I stepped back to admire the neatness, the museum restored. Four years later, unable to reach the shelving and return the Christmas tree stand to its off-season place, come warm weather I rented a dumpster the size of a New York garbage scow and filled it to the max.

Another three years have passed. The warm weather isn't come full force yet, but the snow is gone. Even as I type this I swear I just saw the disrepaired chicken tractor over behind the corn crib creep a foot nearer the pole barn, drawn by the specific gravity inherent in the structure. The last time I went down there it was to get the chainsaw, a process which required a combination of excavation, sideways walking, and general spelunking. Come warm weather, it is once more unto the breach.

It occurs to me just now that based on the formula I have proposed above, the cleaner those pole barns get, the greater the danger that I may be struck by incoming objects...our trash can, the neighbor's combine, a dwarf star. As a precaution I will wear a hard hat and leave a couple of busted lawn mowers, a roll of unusable fencing, and several half-empty cans of 10W-30 motor oil in the corners as a buffer against the implacable forces already at work even as you toss the busted lamp toward the dumpster but feel it bending slowly back toward you on an arc of light and time.

ROLLER SKATE AGAIN

Last week I put my carcass on roller skates for the second time in two years. Me on roller skates is a bad idea for any number of reasons—aesthetics, orthopedics, and physics chief among them—but in both instances there was a child's birthday involved and duty called.

I have a fairly solid roller-skating background, having once served in a professional capacity as a roller-skating Snoopy. While I was never one of those hotshots who could do spins or leaps or win the limbo contest or cut a sweet arc while riding only on my heel wheels, there was a time when I could cruise the rink in a passable manner, any flaws in my technique obscured by my parachute pants and excellently flowing mullet. Unfortunately, "there was a time" was quite specifically 1986, and while my skating skills have not gone completely the way of the Pontiac Fiero, at this point the world is better served by keeping both the Fiero and me off wheels.

But the birthday child will remember the event long after I am gone, so I laced up the tan leather rentals with the unaligned orange wheels and merged wobbily into the flow of traffic beneath the giant disco ball. As the speedsters and youngsters whizzed past it occurred to me that for the safety of all involved I should be wearing an orange construction cone in the manner of a dunce cap.

In roller skating, the bicycle effect applies (once you learn to ride...) and by the third or fourth lap I was motoring along in relative stability. In fact the primary impediment to my trying any fast moves or flourishes had less to do with skills than with the accumulation of knowledge over time as it relates to the long-term effects of concussion, the under-valued joy of an un-bruised coccyx, and the cold reality of four-figure health insurance deductibles.

Nonetheless, having not run straight into a wall and thus feeling emboldened, I attempted to switch from forward-skating to backward-skating. I wound up on the floor. Not a single Samaritan stopped to help—not even those gigglers whose roller skates and health insurance *I paid for*. Lurching back to my feet I quickly diagnosed myself as injury-free, although my ego was showing signs of sprain.

Now my pride kicked in. I got up to speed (well, second gear anyway) and gave it another go. My body reached way back into the archives of muscle memory, and I pulled it off, although unlike the seamless swoop of my youth the move seemed to unfold in ponderous stages, not unlike what you might see should an orangutan suffering an inner ear distur-bance attempt ballet in high heels on an icy sidewalk.

But the birthday girl loved it, and there I was, in one of those beautiful middle-aged moments when you quit caring how you appear and focus on what you intend, which in this case was to demonstrate that Dad was not afraid to play the fool for fun and in fact can do so while roller skating backward.

CHICKEN FENCE

As soon as I hit "send" on this column, I will pull on my rubber boots and head outside to peel the orange plastic safety fence from atop the garlic beds, because the green tops have grown through the latticework to the point of entanglement, and because I promised my wife I would do it before dinner and I like dinner.

We laid the safety fence (in short salvaged sections) atop the beds and pinned it in place with electric fence posts after stuffing the beds with cloves last autumn. Otherwise the chickens—given 37 acres to work with—make a beeline for that one tiny patch and claw the whole works up. Twenty unobserved minutes, and it looks like a garlic grenade went off. You will hear folks extolling the virtues of free range chickens, and how chickens can help tend the garden, keep it free of bugs and whatnot. I don't want to start any fights I can't finish, but let's just say everyone needs limits, including chickens. You give them free range, they strip the chard, chiffonade the basil, and drop mock bubblegum sculptures all over the stoop (rhymes with...).

So fences are in order, and we have them: one encircling

the garden, and a portable one containing the chickens. The fault in this plan lies in the fact time has taken its toll on both enclosures. The one guarding the garlic has become crushed and discontinuous for various reasons over time (including but not limited to an incident involving a brush hog and operator error) and while repairs have been long scheduled they have not been executed. Why are you looking at me?

The portable chicken fence, on the other hand, has developed certain inefficiencies in the form of holes and bent posts, and to make a long story short, I have run out of bungee cords. Then, in the department of exacerbation, spring arrived somewhere around February, meaning both the chickens and the garlic have been out and about way ahead of schedule. In fact, there is some concern about how the garlic will turn out, since the mild winter resulted in a couple of false-start sprouts. Our garlic patch normally yields gloriously fat heads (you could swing one by the braids and knock out a burglar), but who knows what these odd weather rhythms will wreak.

For now, however, the tops are twisting steadily out of the earth and must be freed from the flat plastic fencing. To that end, I am about to put on my boots and get out there. I have a plan and it is this: First, pull up the safety fence, trying not to pull up the garlic with it. In other words, try not to be a big dumb chicken. Then, in a genius move of solving a problem by putting it off, I will take the good sections of portable chicken fence and stake them around the garlic beds, creating a poultry-proof perimeter. The main thing is, I'll get dinner. Although as my wife pointed out immediately after I briefed her on the plan and she stopped rolling her eyes, you're still gonna wanna step carefully coming up the sidewalk.

RUNNER'S WORLD

There is trouble ahead. Five kilometers ahead. Assuming I make it that far.

My younger daughter has recently been participating in an after-school running program. The program culminates in a family "fun run." The "culminating" is now three weeks out. I have been in training for several months now, but the results have been disappointing, in part perhaps because I haven't yet managed to get out for an actual run, fun or otherwise.

Realizing last week that things had kinda snuck up on me, I embarked on a short-term, last-gasp Spartan fitness program that so far has included a renewed dedication to my treadmill desk, stern mirror talks (usually *after* dessert), Tupperware filled with chopped celery and other fat-and-soul-free nibble distractions, a sugar embargo (*embargo* being French for *sieve*), and really focusing on firing my glutes and calves when I climb the eight grueling uphill steps to my office. I also bought a Bluetooth heart monitor to keep me from over-revving when I do finally take that run. Apparently simply wearing it during chair naps or while watching golf doesn't knock much off your lap time. Sadly and also, it tracks you back and forth to the refrigerator.

There was a time I was relatively fleet of foot, but time is a trick mirror, and does nothing for me now (just ask my hairline). It is my understanding that this pending fun run is a "5K" which is a blithe way of saying "short enough you can make it, long enough you won't look good doing so." "5" stands for "Five" and "K" stands for "Kilometers," an imaginary unit of measurement (what is this, Canada?) which taken in quintiplicate equals just over three miles. This distance is doable, but in no way is it "fun."

But: The children. When I pick my daughter up after her sessions she is invariably rosy-cheeked and happy, eagerly reporting her accumulated laps. She also gets string cheese after every practice. Come the big "fun run" day, I would like one of these every "K" if possible. People at tables, handing them out pre-peeled, like miniature dairy-based relay batons. Commemorative t-shirts are nice, but string cheese is a miracle. Would it be so wrong to deep-fry them and include a little plastic cup of dipping sauce? Is it wrong to dip string cheese in melted cheese?

I am off track. I must bear down. Focus on "achieving my goals," as we so often hear we must. Right now my treadmill desk says I have logged 5.74 miles for the day. It is not even noon. Mind you, that's at an average speed of 2.2 miles per hour, which puts me across the "fun run" finish line in just under an hour and a half, Central Slogging Time. I will need to augment my training base with some speedwork. I will begin immediately, with a lumbering wind sprint, proceeding at all speed and not letting up until I get to the kitchen, where lunch awaits.

GROOVY GLASSES

Having settled solidly into that age where reading glasses are a necessity, I find myself unexpectedly backed into a corner I am equipped to neither occupy nor defend: Fashion.

I care not a whit what style readers I wear around the farm, house, and office and regularly prove it. For computer work I have a pair of durable steel-framed safety-style readers. This is kinda like wearing logging boots for your dance recital, and the big lenses give me a look of perpetual surprise and befuddlement, but I have stood on them with said logging boots at least twice and they bend right back into almost-shape without snapping, so victory, even if in their rehabbed state they ride ever more askew, which ups the befuddlement-face factor. My longest-surviving pair are tropically multi-colored and left in the house years ago by my mother-in-law. These work just fine until I answer the door to talk strategy with the septic tank guy and forget I'm wearing them.

Eventually, however, my self-employment requires that I read in public before the public, and I am just vain enough to care how I appear. A lot of the minimally-framed buy'em-by-the-bucket readers look bad on me because I have a head the circumference of a bloated honeydew. By the time the bows reach my ears they are splayed so far as to make it look as if the glasses were first placed on a normal-sized cranium, which was then inflated for the Macy's Thanksgiving Day Parade.

Frameless readers temper the fathead issue by presenting my head and face as they are without obstruction, but this style tends to disintegrate upon touch, and will not survive being sat on or clawed off my face by my godson at Christmas.

Last year while shopping for all-purpose drywall screws (drywall for some of you, all-purpose for the rest of us) in a certain locally-based nationwide big box home improvement store I came across a bin of fashion readers being sold dead-cheap and three to a carton. The most remarkable thing here was that despite being sold within (blurry) view of chop saws, lag bolts, and NASCAR caps, the frames on these glasses were of a horn-rimmed style perfect for scoping out the foam on your macchiato.

For under five dollars, I took a fashion chance. When I wore them in public the first time, I felt a little uncomfortable. In general the image projected was of a befuddled (common theme) farmer-type caught wearing a hempen man-satchel containing vintage fountain pens and hand-stitched writing journals. But no one snickered, and my head didn't look like a distended pumpkin. Emboldened, I next tried a pair with stylish (as in what we used to call "clunky") but *transparent* rims. Kinda Andy Warhol-ish.

I checked them in my phone. I really liked how they looked. I wore them into the house. One by one my wife, my teenaged daughter, and a dear family friend turned to look at me. "Um," said my wife. "Those are...," said the family friend. "Yah...*no*," said my daughter.

I retreated to my room above the garage, where I am understood. There was a knock on the door. It was a dear friend of long acquaintance. By way of greeting, he said, "Dude. Those glasses..." A beat of silence followed. We know each other well enough there was no need to be polite, but he tried. "They're...they're *something*."

When you see me, then, pawing squintfully through the eyewear bin beside the radial arm saws, please respect my privacy on this journey to fashion, currently stranded somewhere between logging boots and lattes.

ASPARAGUS AGAIN

The asparagus isn't coming up right, but I'm glad it's coming up at all. We have two patches, both of them up against the old granary. Today I picked the first batch, nine fine shoots, all from the same clump.

There are no others in sight.

We did everything right last year. Mulched, gave the beds cover for the winter. Covered the mulch with a chicken wire frame to keep the chickens from scratching it up. But even last spring we'd noticed a change. Noticed that rather than all coming up at once the asparagus seemed to come up in shifts. It was nice in the sense that it drew the season out a bit, and we weren't buried all at once, but we also noticed that in some spots it didn't come up at all.

Perhaps some of the wiggly-waggle weather we've had over the past couple of winters has disrupted things. Winter coming and going and (this year) going early. Perhaps there is some sort of mystery asparagus killer out there we're not aware of. Perhaps we overmulched or underweeded or maybe things are fine and I'm just being impatient.

Asparagus seems to be one of those foods that we circle

warily in childhood but come to love as adults. At least that's how it happened for me. Then again my tastes are not infallible, as I also—ever since I first had it at grandma's house—love mushy canned asparagus. This is not the sort of thing a guy should admit in public, I suppose, but I am trying for honesty in all things, and canned asparagus is a place to start.

In the additional category of things one perhaps shouldn't say loudly down to the feed mill, I was once served asparagus truffle foam in a restaurant where someone else was picking up the tab, and it turns out I *like* asparagus truffle foam. I mean, you're gonna wanna supplement it with maybe some beef sticks and cheese before you try to do anything strenuous, like mulching your asparagus beds, but as a one-off treat, it was pretty tasty.

There will be no asparagus foam here (unless I back into the patch with the mower again). Those nine spears are in a mason jar over there on the counter, keeping fresh until they wind up in a skillet or on the grill. Tomorrow I'll wander out to see if any more have poked out of the earth and into the light. Perhaps I'm misreading or misremembering last year's asparagus. I often operate with more certainty than accuracy. In fact, having stated earlier that we don't like asparagus until we are older, I just now recall that I have a daughter still in grade school who has been known to eat the stuff raw, something my wife discovered when she went out to pick the first shoots last year and found them already snapped and the daughter happily chomping.

In the end, I revisit my opening line and realize: The asparagus isn't coming up *wrong*, it's just not coming up as I'd hoped. But we will take what we can get, pleased that the sun is tracking back toward us, bringing with it fresh food and fresh starts.

MILLION BILLION

The bucket of my undeserved blessings overflows like the basement of our house after last week's rains, so what follows is neither a wish nor want list but rather an exercise in fantastical unlikelihood, but: Sometimes I stare out the window at the back forty and wonder what it would be like to have—as my tot once said—a million-billion dollars.

For starters I would buy all the other back forties and just let them sit there. My logger friends are always telling me I should log my back forty (truth in nonfiction: it's just a shade over a back thirty-seven), my farmer friends tell me I should plow or graze it, my developer friends tell me I should develop it, but I like the idea of buying all available acreage adjacent and just letting it sit there without me "improving" it at all.

Almost immediately, though, I backtrack. Because boy-oh-boy if I had that kinda cash, real up high on the wanna list would be one of them rubber-tracked skid-steers outfitted with an articulating brush cutter attachment. I'd cut trails every whichway and once the leaf confetti and sawdust settled I'd get out there and enjoy the silence of nature for a good twenty seconds before heading out to do a little pro bono work for the county. My wife already knows how badly I want one of these multidirectional sapling blitzers, and based on the look she gives me every time I bring it up, I suspect it is she who has been sabotaging all my million-billion-dollar schemes thus far.

Despite this, and to be the bigger person, I'd also buy my wife whatever she wanted, including an airplane ticket to somewhere without me for a week. She has earned this reprieve. No wait, I forgot: I have a million-billion dollars. I'll just rent a jet and buy her an island paved with yoga mats. And then, to prove that money *can* buy you love, I'll hire someone to remind me to close *both* of the porch doors, not leave my toothpicks lying around, and stop treating the laundry basket on the stairs like a hurdle.

Whoops, marital property laws—it occurs to me just now that what's hers is mine and what's mine is hers, and so if you get right down to brass calculators, I have *half* a million-billion dollars. I shall have to adjust the budget.

Still, there will be plenty left over for me to buy a new radial arm saw, which I want because that one I've got now, when you hit the "on" switch, nothing happens, and you gotta run it back and forth forever before you even scratch that two-by-four. I would also like to buy a shed filled with gray socks so I never have to buy socks again and can wash them with whatever I want and any two will make a pair.

I would not spend the money on: fancy guitars (not allowed unless you can *play* fancy), fancy cars (I treat my vehicles like a used van and therefore should be limited to used vans), fancy shoes (but I will go to the Farm & Fleet and get WHATEVER I WANT), or dance lessons (I may have half a million-billion, but I don't wanna *waste* it).

I would love to extend this list. I've barely started spending. But checking the clock and my real bank account, I see it is time to get back to work. The basement leaks but the roof does not. I have sufficient riches.

SLOWFOOT

In fifth grade, I found out I wasn't that fast.

Hopes were high. I figured myself easily set for a top three finish in the hundred-yard dash, and if not that, the forty. Perhaps both. I envisioned the blue—possibly red—ribbons tacked to the corkboard in my bedroom. At that stage in my career I was an academic overachiever (this status peaked around seventh grade) and I somehow assumed this would translate to the track.

It was not to be so. I recall churning futilely as several of my classmates motored past. Harley Paulsrud (name slightly changed to spare him being challenged to footraces in his 50s) was no surprise—we all knew he was fast from freeze tag at recess. But when a kid who went to the special reading classroom and was never picked for flag football or included in our jabbering hangouts shot by me to finish in the top three I remember being startled in a most petulant and unpretty way. As if acing the spelling test and ingratiating myself to the jabberers had earned me fleet feet. As if that kid deserved to be slower. I recall the visceral gut-sink where disappointment met reality. I was also self-conscious in front of my teacher, who I admired and who had just witnessed me in failure.

What an important day that was. In the most benign way, it imposed reality on my dreams and my ego. It prepared me to meet people who are more talented than I, both within and without my areas of expertise. Who write more beautifully than I. Who sell more books than I. People who understand electricity, or turn the wrench in the right direction the first time, or buy the right spark plug on the first try. People who come outta nowhere and beat me at my own game.

Later, in high school, I discovered distance running. Turns out while I was a slo-mo sprinter I had decent ability in the mile. At my peak I could run it in under five minutes. I learned what it felt like to cross the finish line first now and then. I even won a conference championship. But just up the road from me were two other runners named Koll and Al. We went to different schools and were in different conferences, but we trained together. Every day in practice their times were better than mine. Every time we ran I trailed them. At the end of the season, I would finish first or second in my regional competition and move to sectionals, where I would face off with Koll and Al, who had finished one-two in their regional. Only the top two finishers in sectionals went to state. Every year I watched from the final turn as Koll and Al crossed the line ahead of me. I knew I had trained and run as hard as I could. I knew there are some distances all the visualization and extra miles and positive thinking in the world won't bridge. That sometimes losing isn't losing—no, wait, it *is* losing—but in losing you can gather information. And not quit, but rather tighten your focus. Arrive at the finish line long after the string is snapped, but stay on pace, looking for another race.

GREEN DAYS

The speed at which spring redoubles when given a chance is startling. There is that period of warming during which the color emerges rather than explodes: The countryside "greens up," there are sprouts and buds and catkins dropping, and things are moving modestly along...then one day the lawn is eight inches high and you can't see the firewood chunks alongside the driveway that you've been meaning to get to since the snow melted and you were reminded you were meaning to get to them last fall.

In the time it took for the June bugs to emerge from the dirt, the hostas have gone from spiky to salad bowl thick. The pale flittering maple leaflets are suddenly full, dark, and draping from the stem. The burdock are pushing their jade elephant ears between everything else and the sun, their palmy softness breezily shifting and dipping, a dismissive fan dance distraction meant to buy time for the prickly burrs incubating elsewhere in the chlorophyll. The nettles are stemming up, the orchard grass clumps are top-knotty. Suddenly, the celeriac would fill a silo.

Even as the green reaches this thickness, there are signs it won't last. Down the road, the real farmer has already dropped some hay. He is compelled by his cows, and knows that just as quickly as the green peaks, so can the quality. I would say he is unconstrained by poetry, but that is to short-change any farmer who has learned to grade forage by the scanning the timothy heads, or judging the timbre of the stem-crack. We are all readers.

By raising and experience there is just enough of the farmer in me to recognize the privilege I have stumbled into that I might be allowed for one more season to stand beneath the sun and absorb all this green. To be spared even for a moment from all tumult to take in this time when there is emerald beauty to be found even in the box elder. When the wild cucumber is still tentative, spikeless and not yet set to strangling. When the quack grass tastes sweet.

But we are by self-imposed definition civilized. So we move into the season of cutting. Of the mower, the weed-whacker, the hand scythe, the thistle-whip, the brush hog. Even a groundskeeper as lax as I makes some concessions to walking paths, chicken pasture, croquet space, and access to the lumber pile. But before you pull the start cord, as you run the stone along the blade, when you're cracking open the clamshell that holds the whip string, perhaps you pause and look out the shed door, take one last moment to see the world as it is, hung in this balance, as we wish it might always be: Green, simply green.

ST. JUDE

Somewhere around the age of forty-two, I hit that stage where more and more I recognized recurrent patterns of behavior in humanity in general and myself in particular. This workaday predictive ability solves pretty much nothing and in fact remains a regular source of frustration and pique, but the upshot is, it makes life more navigable. Good or bad, you sense what's coming, and which way to steer. It isn't that you can avoid the collision, but you buy yourself time to brace, or assume a position designed to minimize collateral damage. It isn't a crystal ball type of insight. It's more a low-grade prescience. You look at something the younger you would have accepted at face value, solve for the variables of human nature, and shortly extrapolate a narrow range of how things are gonna go.

Lately these instincts have been failing me. Not completely: I've been right about a lot of things I wish I'd gotten wrong. But it also turns out I've severely underestimated the power of mendacity. Socially speaking, we live in a time of blunt instruments.

I have nothing original to say on the subject, and indeed

am most effective when I stick to my wheelhouse: benign domestic mishaps, wry asides, cow references, my incompetence with hand tools. The occasional reflective vignette featuring a tire swing or the hay balers of yesteryear. Every day—today included—I am grateful to be allowed this little life of mine. Apart from high school football and basic firefighting I've never been a good frontline battler, and admire those who are. Those who lead the way, articulate in defense of truth and goodness. But every day I question if my less-fortunate neighbors can rely on me.

From my desk I can see a laminated prayer card featuring the image of St. Jude. I bought it for a dollar at the Dickeyville Grotto in Southwestern Wisconsin while researching a book based on *pareidolia*, a psychological phenomenon that explains why people see Jesus in a grilled cheese sandwich, or the Blessed Virgin Mary in a pizza. The card is wedged between the wall and the window frame. Available in case of emergency. Sometimes when things aren't going so well I pull out the songwriter Drew Nelson's "Tilt-A-Whirl" album and stare at that card while Track Four plays on repeat:

> *in the moonlight, I am praying*
> *to the patron saint of fools*
> *in the darkness my supplication*
> *would you light my way St. Jude*

The muted fingerpicking, the chill organ note—each imply quietude in the face of brute force. Surrender as sweet victory. Sweetest of all? That word, *supplication*. Reminding me how I still love the terms of faith upon which I was raised. *Supplication*. To ask. To beg. To know humility.

St. Jude. The patron saint of fools. Of desperate situations. Of lost causes. I figure right about now he's running out of business cards and has hired extra help to answer the phones. I have no trumpet to blow here—like so many I just need to get the work done and keep my kids fed. Next week I'll do my best to lighten up. Maybe write about the wrens nesting in my air conditioner, or how I stubbed my gouty toe. But for now I'm sitting with St. Jude, recalibrating the narrow range of how things are gonna go.

DAD SOCKS

Today I went to town wearing shower flip-flops over gray socks. This was pointed out to me in public by an acquaintance I had not anticipated encountering. "Nice *dad* look," he said, and I couldn't disagree, as in fact I had my ten-year-old daughter in tow. I nearly told him I had chosen the flip-flops in the tender wake of a big-toe gout-bout, but there is little nobility in gout, and in fact I was now nearly pain-free and motivated more by laziness and sunshine. Why then bother with socks? Well, who but a podiatrist wants to see a recovering gouty toe?

I just smiled and said, "Yep, I have happily surrendered."

"I'm still working on that," he said, implying that he hasn't, and won't. He too is a dad, but fresher to the game than I. I figure by the time he has a teen driver I'll catch him in the grocery store buying kitty litter and toilet paper in his bathrobe.

I can wait.

In truth I gave up on dressing for approval years ago, but I am also pursuing an ulterior motive: Embarrassing the offspring.

Children deserve love and respect and arms to hold them, but they also deserve to know that not all happiness is found atop the pop charts, in the mirror, or on the clothes rack at the mall. What better way to let them know this than to embarrass them by shedding your own sense of embarrassment? Whenever any random pop song comes on the radio in the car I light up and say, "Is this the *Biebs?!?*" just to hear the groans. I regularly announce that I dipped into one of the multitude of hair products crowding my teensy corner of the bathroom countertop in order to thicken the sparse crop atop my gleaming pate just to bathe in the synchronized eye-rolls.

And I haul them off to town while wearing gray socks and flip-flops.

Somehow—so far—it works out. They cringe, but they realize that despite my lagging—nay, *lumbering*—behind the cultural curve, I still manage to be relatively happy and fulfilled in what I do. And that if I'm not wearing the right brand of pants I am nonetheless available with those arms of mine in times of tears.

When we got back into the van, my ten-year old asked what the man meant. I told her he was poking fun at me for wearing gray socks and flip-flops in public. "Dad," said the child, "you *rock* that look." I allowed myself a smile, but it was only half formed when she said, "Because you dress like that all the time!"

Well now. That was a little more ambiguous. It also just now occurs to me that perhaps I haven't given enough thought to what my wife thinks of me wandering around looking like I just left the porch looking for a newspaper. Just because I can contort my sartorial slackness into a child-rearing technique doesn't mean she deserves to be seen in public with a schlub. Resolved: The next time she and I visit the city I'll wear a nice pair of shoes. Or at the very least my nicest pair of logger boots. The ones with the safety tips. In defense of the gouty toe.

CARDINALS

This morning the gray rainscape was brightened by the sight of a dusky red mother cardinal pecking across the driveway outside my driveway window. She was flanked by a pair of birds her same size. They were tan and of similar configuration. It took me a moment to realize they were her offspring. The clincher came when she turned toward one and it gawped its face wide open. The mother popped her beak down the youngster's gullet and deposited whatever it was she had pecked off the damp pavement.

On she hopped and on she pecked, the children tagging close behind. Every few feet she stopped, turned, and stuffed one or the other maw. In light of their size the younger birds looked ludicrous not fending for themselves. I was reminded of adolescents wandering helplessly through a well-stocked kitchen, waiting for hamburgers to drop from the light sockets and string cheese to pour out the faucets.

It lightened my heart to see the youngsters thriving, however. Last year a robin laid eggs in a nest not three feet off the ground in a spruce tree down by the pole barn, and while my younger daughter enjoyed checking the eggs, she got a dose of cold nature when a windstorm upended the whole works before hatching, leaving nothing but a frayed nest and chips of eggshell blue in the grass. Another robin has nested in the yard this year, a good fifteen feet up in a young but sturdy maple. I can't see the eggs, but I can see her up there resolutely set. So far, so good.

Then there were the wrens who built a nest in my office window, packing a narrow space between the sill and air conditioner with sticks and pine needles (and, I am told by the internet, spider egg sacs...excuse me while I check my office chair and shudder). It was a bad place for a nest but they had it well homesteaded by the time I discovered them, and over the next few weeks I came to love their burbling song—such bright noise from such brown birds—although I had to work hot because every time I turned the air conditioner on, Mama wren fled. I'd rather be sweaty than guilty, so I rationed my cool-downs. Two days ago I heard a thump and the wrens scolding. When I exited the office a cat was hanging by both forepaws from the windowsill, the nest was pulled apart, and a barely-feathered wren chick was weakly waving its wings. Before I could intervene the chick was eaten.

The following day I hung a wren house within view of the office window. Amends, I suppose. Or hope. I enjoyed writing to wrensong and hope I may again. Birds and baby birds in springtime are a lesson in acceptance. Nature makes no investment in care or kindness. Your garden variety bird survives on determination and chance. The father cardinal and his bright red feathers, for whatever reason, are nowhere to be seen.

SUGAR BOMBS

Today I awoke sharply at 4 a.m. because my wife was jabbing me in the shoulder. Apparently someone in the room was snoring and had disturbed her. I don't know what she expected me to do about it, so I went back to sleep. Or tried. I kept waking myself up with the sound of my own...snoring.

I blame it on a sore throat and itchy ears. These symptoms appeared sometime after midnight. Over the course of 52 years I have retained my tonsils and adenoids (and a festering jealousy toward my brother John, who had his out when we were young and as a result was allowed to eat extracurricular ice cream in the hospital) so perhaps they had become inflamed and caused some sort of audible nasopharyngeal turbulence sufficient to wake my wife. (I try to use words like "nasopharyngeal" whenever possible as a return on an early investment, specifically a four year nursing degree I used for under two years.)

As a general rule (and with a hearty knock on wood—I assume nothing) I don't get sick much. This is a source of regular consternation to my wife, as she is dietarily well-disciplined, exercises daily, and does her best to encourage me in the same direction. I respond by eating my vegetables and doing some desultory treadmilling.

This time, however, I think I know what happened, and it's embarrassing. Having shorted myself on sleep for the better part of two weeks and finding myself with one more deadline finish line to cross before I could let up, I turned to my favorite performance enhancing drug after caffeine—sugar. I didn't shoot it or snort it, but I certainly mainlined it, right down my dumb gullet. The delivery mechanisms took many forms, but I'd say the final overdose came in the form of a bag of lemon sugar cookies and another of chocolate peanut clusters bought in a local store that sells things in bulk (which, coincidentally, is exactly how I ate them).

When, in the wee hours of the morning, I finished the project, all but a few of the cookies and clusters remained. Also—let's just get this out into the open—half a bag of chocolate-coated kiwi fruit. Honestly, you really haven't come to terms with your own self-loathing until you've binged on chocolate-coated kiwi fruit. I mention it here as a form of penance and in hopes that the shame will carry over into my next run of deadlines and save me from myself.

Anyway, based on what my wife has tried to teach me about sugar, I believe I left myself immunologically compromised, and now I have a sore throat, a cough, and my wife has a snoring problem. I have been here before, and as usual have embarked on an ascetic course of drastic self-improvement. Last night the family stopped for ice cream at a local shop. I sampled one marble-sized dollop, then sat there piously, thinking I wonder if you can get your tonsils out one at a time, because I am getting cheated out of a lot of ice cream here.

SPITWAD

Whither the spitwad?

The question arose this morning when I discovered a Bic Cristal pen on my desk. Prior to this I simply knew it as the pen we all used in late grade school, when we were allowed to move beyond the fat pencil. Nowadays we can research these things online, and in addition to the fancy name I learned this particular model was launched in 1950 and has since become the bestselling pen in the world. In fact it is described as "ubiquitous" although if I was in charge, it would be described as "u-Bic-uitous." If someone in the Bic marketing department wants to contact me I'll be happy to tell you where to send the checks.

I used to covet—even hoard—Bic Cristal pens. They were my favorite doodle utensil. They rarely failed, and even when they did you could use your teeth to pull the brass tip and attached ink tube, then clamp your lips around the non-writing end of the tube, blow puff-cheek hard, and force the ink to flow again. On the downside I once witnessed an act of elementary vandalism committed by a ne'er-do-well who detached the tip and blew ink across a teacher's white coat.

In the wrong hands, everything's a weapon.

Another attraction of this particular model of Bic was the cap, which consisted of plastic just malleable enough to be chewable. In fact, as a public service announcement, I credit my strong teeth to a regular regimen of adolescent pen cap gnawing. That one's yours pro bono, American Dental Association.

But mainly when I saw that pen this morning I thought of spitwads. I wish to neither glorify nor precipitate spitwads—teachers face enough hindrance as it is—but I wondered if the advent of so many screens has caused a drop-off in the amount of children chewing up notebook paper and flinging it. I sat in the back of the English room with Harley Paulsrud, and he could gob up big old wads that would stick to the ceiling, but then he was a professional, having had many hours in detention to refine his technique. Most kids flicked little white specks. The clock in our high school English room was barely readable for all the dried pulp peppering its face.

But if you really wanted to put one in someone's ear three rows over, you needed a Bic Cristal. You removed the cap, then pulled the brass tip and ink tube. Next you undid the countersunk cap covering the butt end. This often required gnawing, but you were already in good practice for that. Next you ripped chunks of paper from your spiral notebook, gave them a good chewing, and then, removing a BB-sized gob from the ammo magazine of your cheek, deposited it in the empty hexagonal barrel (perhaps using the ink tube to tamp it down like a mini-muzzle loader). After selecting your target, allowing for distance and windage and being sure the teacher's back was turned, you covered the pinhole on the side of the barrel, and blew a short, sharp puff. If your aim was true, some studious person would snap upright, swiping madly at the nape of their neck. By this time your weapon would have been stowed and you would be carefully reviewing your preposition list.

I briefly considered deconstructing my Bic and test-firing it this morning, but there was work to be done. In truth I rarely shot spitwads in school. How did I learn so much about the craft? I say only this: Blessed are those who instigate, for they can let Harley Paulsrud take all the heat.

TENDING GARLIC

This year the garden ran heavy to garlic, which is to say we didn't plant anything else. For purposes of definition, "we" includes me, as I poked a few bulbs into the dirt last fall and helped with a little weeding, but these beds—and this garden—has overall been tended and brought into long-term fertility by my wife. The mulching, the turning, the mounding, the enriching of the earth, this is all her work over the course of many years.

There are things you think you'll always do. In the waning years of my bachelorhood I took to gardening. I was mediocre at it, but I enjoyed it, and always got a lot of fresh herbs and some tomatoes out of the deal. Then we got married, other work and family commitments expanded, and before long I hadn't made my favorite roast tomato stock for a decade. This same tapering off has occurred in other areas of formerly profound commitment: bicycle racing, fishing, Tarzan books...certitude.

In general I accept this. We change, we grow. We grow, we change. Loyalty, fidelity, faithfulness, reliability, dedication... these are all critically important traits, but left unexamined can permute into brittleness. Sometimes we simply move on. No drama, no significance, just transition. I never got sick of bike racing, I just decided to devote my time to other pursuits. I occasionally miss it, I never crave it.

In other cases—fresh herbs, for instance—we hold out hope that we'll circle back. I would like one day to have some pigs snuffling about outside my office as I did the first few years of our life on this old farm. I should like, before I draw my last breath, to spend some long hours in a boat catching —or not catching—fish. I'd like to write poems at the pace of my youth. I am not desperate to do these things—in this full life I have so much to be grateful for—but I am not ready to let go the thread of possibility.

The garlic is our garden's thread. In a year when work and family calendars predicted we'd never keep the usual beans and peas and carrots and potatoes and kale and Swiss chard and whatever else all watered and weeded from first turn to harvest, we settled for just the garlic. It felt like giving up, it felt like letting go, it is what it is, no drama. We've already gathered the scapes, and now the tops are going brown, so we'll pull the plants soon, arrange them on the rack to dry in the kiln of the steel pole barn. We are interested in getting a peek at the bulbs, as the roller coaster mildness of last autumn and early winter combined with a record early false spring resulted in some premature sprouting. Until we shake them free of the dirt, until we slice the first, we won't know how they were affected.

In the meantime, we'll go about our summer. Perhaps next year we'll dive back into greens and vegetables. Certainly this autumn   health and circumstance allowing— we'll press some of this year's bulbs back in the ground, then see what next year brings. Turn the earth, and let the earth turn.

AFTER THE WINDS

July, and it looks like green autumn out there this morning. The lawn is littered with leaves. A ragged scatterplot of windfalls lie beneath the apple tree, unreddened. A maple branch went down and took the clothesline with it. Another is partially blocking the drive. The back door of the chicken coop blew open. This I didn't discover until I went out to let the chickens out at dawn only to find them clustered at the feed pan. I should like to say they greeted me but in fact they just blinked beadily. After a blustery night they wanted food, not affection.

The winds swept through in the wake of a thunderstorm storm rather than before it. This was unusual enough that the local meteorologist devoted a side segment to it in his report. He had a specific term for such winds, but I failed to write it down so it has blown away for now. I could of course ask my phone, but sometimes these days I'm content not knowing everything.

The clothesline is a bummer. It's one of the few handyman projects I've ever fully completed. It runs from the deck railing to the woodshed. Pulleys on both ends so we can stand on the deck and run the laundry back and forth. Plastic-coated green wire that reminds me of the wires I used to see running along the railroad tracks of my youth. Which in turn reminds me of the heavy glass insulators my mom placed in rows along the windowsills of our farmhouse. A collector stood in the kitchen once and told her they were worth money but even though we could have used the cash Mom just smiled, perhaps already knowing that forty years later my recollection of the bright light of day slowing and cooling as it passed through the blue-green glass would even now lower my blood pressure.

The clothesline will have to be repaired. The two fallen limbs must be cut up and dragged off, at least the brushy ends too small to be chunked and split for firewood. The midsized limbs will be gathered up by the resident grade-schooler as a means of reinforcing our much-ballyhooed American work ethic, specifically the subcategory of Working While Grumpy. The mower will mulch the rest.

The chickens are all accounted for, despite being at the mercy of varmints. Based on our nocturnal driveway traffic this is the season of young skunks and raccoons in training (work ethic, kids!) so it was a nervous accounting and I must add the sprung latch to my list of unhandyman tasks.

All in all, minimal damage. Now the sun is out and bright. Alongside the old granary, tiger lilies hover at the end of their long stems, dipping in light breeze like flocks of blaze-orange Tinkerbells. Many of the pale purple hosta blossoms have been swept groundward, but the hummingbirds are still at them, having simply adjusted their angle of attack. Those insulators were lovely, but sometimes an unfiltered light is best.

CORN

This week's emotional reprieve came in the form of corn.

I had dropped in to visit my neighbor Tom. I was traveling not from my nearby farm but rather from town, where I had just attended an extended meeting that—while it was led by good people for good reasons—was nonetheless overshadowed by the fact that down here at sea level our sails are often shredded by rank and distant winds belched from the mouths of fools.

It was in this state of mind that I turned up Tom's driveway, a dirt two-track running perpendicular to the county road, up a gentle rise, then curving left toward a house and outbuildings hidden behind a ridge. In another vehicle behind me was a farm-raised man who could pass for a lumberjack and in fact knows how to be a lumberjack but has a brain for computers which he turned into the sort of success that could have changed him but didn't, although he drives a pretty nice truck. He had heard my neighbor Tom had a homemade cannon. I had agreed to arrange a meeting.

Much of the corn in these parts has suffered this year. So

much rain, and much of it right after the sprout. Swathes of bare dirt where the runoff swept away the plants that hadn't already drowned. Humpy stands of varying height. And even now in the high sandy spots a few plants starting to twist a bit for want of moisture. But the corn on either side of Tom's drive is standing tall and thriving.

I killed the radio and the air conditioning and rolled the window down, thinking I'd use the quarter mile to air out the van and my head. I wasn't prepared for the sweetness that rushed in. The air was like fine-spun syrup.

The corn, of course. Slipping past the van just beyond my fingertips, warmed to redolence by the afternoon sun. I breathed deeply. Warm-drawn honey. Maybe a touch of cotton candy. I found myself smiling.

We had a good visit with Tom. It's been a while now since he lost Arlene, his wife of 60 years, and lately his eyes have been giving him trouble, but once the stories start flowing he comes alive, spry in stance and spirit. That one about the crooked shovel handle that got bent from the county worker leaning on it, you can see him reveling in it like he never told it a hundred times.

I'd say it took us about two hours to work up to the cannon, but then Tom charged and fired it. You will get a sense of the bore on this weapon if you understand Tom shoots tin stew cans filled with concrete. The boom and blast had the desired effect on the newcomer, who grinned as wide as one can without the help of a dentist. Before we parted we talked about the state of the corn, how when we were young on the farm we'd sneak out into it just for the silence. Nothing but the soft rasp of the leaves. How the tassel-tops overtook the landscape, how at its tallest when it surrounded the yard and buildings the farmstead felt somehow secret, safe, and hidden. I recalled chewing the stalks, the pithy sugar of them. Then Tom went to his house and we went to our vehicles. At the county road it'd be a right angle turn back into reality, so I took my time leaving, driving slowly down the narrow keyway cut through the sweet, sweet green.

CHAINSAW CHAIN

Before I could clear the trails, I had to reassemble the chainsaw. It had been disassembled for use as a prop in a play, which is the sort of situation you may find yourself in if you are a rural-based supporter of the arts.

It is a recurring theme of my life and writing that my mechanical skills are commensurate to my ballet skills: I have a general sense of the moves and you can tell what I'm shooting for, but it just doesn't ever go the way I hope.

But: I was raised by loggers and still comport with them on occasion. I may be a soft-handed typist but I can do the chainsaw basics. In this case, I didn't have to repair anything, just remount the blade, the chain, and the shield. There was one minor delay when I dropped a threaded nut and in trying to catch it with the top of my boot, drop-kicked it into the far corner of the pole barn. This is what happens when cat-like reflexes meet kitten-like coordination.

There came a further delay when I discovered the chain, which had been sliding around loose in a cardboard box, had doubled back on itself several times, creating a series of interlocking loops. Each time I undid one loop, another appeared.

At one point I decided the trick was to snatch the whole thing inside out, like how you'd reach in and reverse an inverted sock, but this had the disappointing effect of turning one loop into two.

Through sheer stubbornness I finally unlooped it. After threading the chain into place, I was itching to get going. Then I thought of my brother the logger, and how he would never set foot outside this shed without sharpening the chain. I pulled out the file and took my time, making a full circuit. I'm never quite sure if I've got the raker teeth right, but nonetheless, as I placed the saw into the tractor bucket, I felt responsible and imagined my brother giving me the thumbs up.

As I swung aboard the tractor I paused, wondering if I should load up extra fuel and oil and my chainsaw tools, but because I would only be zipping up a couple of smallish limbs and trees, I decided to travel light. Ignoring that little *are you sure?* voice, I engaged the power takeoff, goosed the throttle, lowered the brush hog, and set off down the trail.

I was on the farthest forty from the house before I encountered the first fallen log blocking the trail. I dismounted, donned my safety gear, fired up the chainsaw, and set to cutting. I pegged the tree for a maple, but it seemed to be made of iron; no matter how I revved, the saw refused to bite. The rakers? Did I leave them too tall? I checked. They seemed fine. I tried sawing again. Same thing. Just a futile buzz and now a touch of smoke.

I had put the chain on backward, of course. Rather than biting into the wood, the teeth were running dull-end first, beating up the bark but doing little else. Reversing the chain is simple enough. Simply loosen the tensioner, undo two bolts, flip it, and snug everything back up again. Two minutes, tops, and requiring the simplest of tools, a combination wrench/screwdriver. Currently nestled in the toolbox back in the pole barn where I chose to leave it despite the little voice.

The things I said next would not fit in my little voice. But this being the cellular age, I snapped a sweaty angry-face selfie, tagged it with an explanatory caption, and sent it to my brother the real logger. His happy-face response reaffirmed my belief that confession is good for the soul, and in idiocy can be found joy.

COUSIN EDDIE

It is good to have a cousin named Fast Eddie and I have one. If Fast Eddie is from Philly—as my cousin is—all the better. When you come from where I'm from—rural Wisconsin— the idea of someone being from "Philly" reminds you of the movies. Gritty movies. You think of a guy who could maybe punch a side of beef.

In the distant past when Fast Eddie married into our family, I was told he was a railroad conductor in California. I imagined a man with one elbow out a locomotive window, blue-and-white striped engineer's cap snugged down on his skull, red bandana knotted around his throat, the cloth and his beard flowing backward and snapping in the wind as he snaked a mile of cars through a mountain pass. Later he explained he didn't actually sit in the window seat, but the original image stuck, and it took me over a decade's worth of family reunions before I stopped asking him how things were going up there at the front of the train.

These days Fast Eddie—who has stacked up some miles and zip codes over the years—lives in the Nashville area, where our family just spent three days visiting him and his wife, a woman I shall refer to as Cool Breeze.

Over the years my visits with Fast Eddie have been mostly in passing at reunions, weddings, and funerals, with many years between. This recent visit allowed us to spend time walking and driving around Nashville and jawboning late into the night. Turns out Fast Eddie has more history than any old passenger train can hold. Some of it I can share, some of it I can share only if I never want to go to Philadelphia, and most of it I can't share at all. I certainly can't tell you the one about the time he took a break from switching out the engine in his muscle car in order to turn back the odometer on a van owned by a rock star now residing with his Grammys in the sky, a favor that led to backstage access and other freelance opportunities. Can't tell you the one about his first job in 8th grade or whom he worked for, although I will say they were part-time chemists who favored two-wheeled transportation and the boy wasn't running a paper route. I shan't get into the specifics of why he has no interest in returning to Austin, Texas, or why he left that party in the high desert of California early. Or why, should you mention the name "Fast Eddie," a certain pastor in rural Tennessee will fetch up with a twitch in his eye.

What I will tell you is Fast Eddie can walk up to a man thrice his size and invite him to leave with a smile that says *yesterday!* and that big man will go. That Fast Eddie is festooned with tattoos not purchased at standard retail. But that same Fast Eddie will burn three straight days of vacation time just to sit with a neighbor as he grieves. Should you have trouble with your yard light wiring or goons blocking your driveway, Fast Eddie will be of assistance in both respects. Should you need mechanic work Fast Eddie can swap out your transmission in the time it took me to type up this column, although as far as that drywall in the living room, well, Cool Breeze has been asking him to get to that for upwards of a year now.

I keep a little list. About ten names long. The Root-Hog-or-Die list, I call it. Got the phrase from Louis L'Amour. Means trouble has come and must be dealt with in the present moment. Fast Eddie is on that list. May I never have to call him. If I do, I will repay him in secrets and promises kept.

SMOKY MOUNTAINS

Two weeks ago I was in the Smoky Mountains. You move around the country, you move your brain. This is an ever-more essential process. So much sitting in one place, staring at a screen, festering up worries and resentment. Travel broadens your mind, they say, and right they are, although in the process one also comes to wish some folks would never leave their lairs. There is also the ongoing project of my acknowledging certain privileges, travel high among them. Bootstraps talk has long been conflated with shoe leather—why don't you people just pick up and change your situation? These days many of us don't even have to leave our home county to witness the fallacy of that one. Still, it is easier to sit in comfort and cast aspersion upon distant circumstance. But who am I to talk. One more Dad in a Van, preaching at the windshield.

The Smokies, as my ten-year-old noted one morning while fog lolled low between the green ridges, are *smoky*. In fact, less than a year ago they had been swept with real smoke. Wildfires. The denuded and discolored swaths are still visible. Over a dozen people died. Dolly Parton is from around here, and pitched in to help.

We had come to the Smokies to meet family from all around the country. We rented two cabins and stuffed them to overflowing. Played cards, watched favorite movies, passed the stories around, and down. In general it was a happy cacophony. I married into this bunch and happy I am to have done so. There is enough difference among us that certain topics are best given polite berth. So it is all over the place. All the more reason, perhaps, to tend the central threads. Among the bonds of civilization I count second cousins, crowded tables, and cross-generational dishwashing shifts.

Harmony requires we sing different notes, I was going to say, but as with many decoratively stitched pillows that one doesn't really hold up in a fight. I tell my children we travel so we may hear voices freshly, and firsthand. Some we ponder and prefer not to respond. Some we oppose. Others we amplify. Two miles from our cabin there stood a giant bill-board featuring Dolly Parton. On our way out of town I snapped a photo of it and shared it with Dr. Tressie McMillan Cottom, a sociologist at Virginia Commonwealth University. I first encountered Dr. McMillan Cottom on Twitter. The connections linking her and me and Dolly are baroque beyond description in this allotted space, but indeed they arose from travel outside my normal cornpone comfort zone. Online travel, yes, but no matter where we sit our minds are free to go.

Round-trip we covered 2,118 miles. Every day I'd sneak a little time with the news, then lay it like a scrim over what-ever America I saw before me. I'm back home now. It's late August. The meadow grasses are threaded with dead stems. The black cap canes are stripped. The hosta scapes arc like fishing rods leaned against the wall of an empty cabin. Long before autumn arrives, it insinuates itself.

POST-ECLIPSE

The eclipse has passed, and we have returned to ignoring wonder. Even as it was happening there was the temptation to refuse to be caught up in it, to distinguish ourselves from the selfie-blast of grinning fools in cardboard glasses. To roll our eyes rather than roll back our heads. To be too cool to goggle the sun.

Our family is not so good at planning ahead for things. We were on our way home from a trip to Tennessee when a cousin in St. Louis gave us four pair of the glasses, each flat in its plasticine sleeve. I remember thinking, *Well, maybe.*

We are in that stage of life when our family of four often travels in three different directions (Sweet Joy, the teenager is employed!), so when the eclipse commenced, we convened in the parking lot of a beauty salon for an early peek. Those chintzy little glasses worked a treat, and the minute I saw the sun as a dusky tangerine short one crisp nibble, all the jade fell away, and in the selfie I am your grinning fool.

I headed downtown on errands then, the world out the windshield shading off-blue, the breeze across my elbow going noticeably cool as the moon made its move. The atmosphere was odd; neither dark nor nocturnal, just not quite right to the eye, as if a newbie misplayed the Instagram filter.

At the heart of downtown I found my way blocked by sawhorses and people, everybody sungazing. By now the eclipse was peaking. I diverted and found myself driving past my favorite bar, a joint called The Joynt. It seemed as good a place as any. I parked out front, and, standing before the well-worn entry, tipped my head back. The sun was clipped to a crescent. Inside the empty tavern, two barkeeps—one of whom has slung everything but light beer here for decades—were cleaning and prepping. I leaned in. "You guys got goggles?"

"Forgot all about it!" said the veteran. He tucked the cardboard bows in place, had a look, and spoke a joyful word aloud. There will be no direct quote here as the word is multipurpose and heavily dependent on context. Think of it as "Wow!" The second barkeep had a look as well. She said less, but smiled as widely. Then they thanked me for sharing, and returned to their swamping.

At a bar one door down, two beer-bellied beard-bros were poking a hole in a piece of cardboard. "Wanna try these?" I asked, offering the glasses. The bro holding the cardboard hesitated, then accepted them. Each had a look in turn. "Cool!" said the first. "That *is* cool!" said the second.

Just then a longtime artist friend I hadn't seen in years bicycled past. John is legendarily grumpy. I have long said his life's philosophy can be summed up in a single two-word phrase. One of those words is compound, and again, cannot be printed with this ink. "John!" I said, waving the glasses. Still astride his bike, he took them and looked. "Huh," he said. But what a smile he wore as he pedaled away.

As I reached the van, another man—I don't know his circumstance but recognize him as having wandered these streets with a cigarette since I was in college—happened past. "Want a look?" I asked. "Well, yeah," he said. And the snip of sun, starting now to grow again, made him smile too.

It was all over so quickly. There was no stopping it. Today I heard Van Morrison sing, "*Lift me up, consume my darkness,*" and I thought, Yessir, for a few minutes at the very least.

RED SQUIRREL

The person I was to meet this morning is running late, so I'm sitting on a bench in the country outside a locked door. A red squirrel is giving me a good scolding. He's probably right. Perhaps he is working security.

It's 8 a.m. A good time of day for sitting still. The morning come to life for a while now but still fresh. Off to my left—to my north, actually—the grass is a few days removed from its last mowing, neat but no longer flat-topped, frayed with just enough wisp and dew to catch a shimmer from the sun when the breeze brushes by. It's a cool breeze, not cold, and light across the skin, but the subliminal suggestion is it is building up enough puff to flip the calendar page from August to September.

The bench faces a county road that cuts through an area of the county lying along the edge of change: There is no wall-to-wall development, but much of the farmland has been divvied up into lots. The dwellings out here are a blend of old farmhouses, low-slung ranch homes dating to the 60s and 70s, a later vinyl-sided wave of post-millennial construction, and here and there at the end of a curving blacktopped drive, a big honker clearing the seven-figure assessment hurdle. A short mile down the road the township hall and fire department building are sized to another time. Down along the main highway in the corner of a field there is hung a banner requesting more volunteers. The traffic on the road before me consists largely of folks headed for work in the city center twenty minutes away. It occurs to me that this may have something to do with why it's tough to fill seats at the monthly fire meeting. *Things change*, I think. Then I think, *Good one, Captain Obvious*. I regularly have these little talks with myself.

The red squirrel has ceased his hectoring and disappeared. I'm fiddling with my phone, getting set to check some emails, when I realize perhaps my job for the moment is to just sit there. Just see what I can see. What I can hear. Those chickadees, for instance, conversing over by a bank of purple coneflowers. Echinacea, I think that is. I used to take it in tea when I felt a cold coming on. Never came to a firm conclusion regarding its efficacy. If it works for you, terrific.

A spruce tree towers heavily above me. It is hung with pine cones: green, pitch-heavy and dense. Every now and then one drops to the ground with a sodden thud. I am reminded of the apples falling to the lawn back home.

I have a habit of listening to the business news out of New York in the mornings, and I give in to the temptation, tapping my phone and unleashing the stream. Right about the same time, I realize the pine cones are dropping at a steady rate, and now I know where that squirrel went. He's gnawing them off the branch, and will bury them for the winter.

On my phone the contrarians and skeptics are holding forth on the future and futures, but at the moment I am content to sit and draw no conclusions beyond the idea that sometimes the best we can do is simply dwell in time and that squirrel is going to get a solid return on his investment.

BACHATA

There are many ways to listen. Last week I wrote of listening to the morning as it was brought to me by birds. Today I write of listening to music as it was brought to me through earplugs.

It still sounded good.

Ours is a bilingual family in a number of respects. This is traceable to rural high school exchange programs, immigration, marriage, hope, hard work, and, in my case, flash cards. You do not want me translating anything important. Once in Panama I ordered ice and got Oreos.

The trip this time required no international travel, only that we drive a few hours south to a spot outside Mauston, where music fans by the thousands were gathering for the two-day Los Dells Festival. Thanks to family get-togethers and some old CDs I was familiar with some of the music and acts prior, but contemporary bachata and reggaetón not being in my primary wheelhouse, I had done some homework, discovering—among other things—that some among us (specifically, two out of three people in the minivan) were very eager to be entertained by a young man known as Prince Royce.

We met our relatives at their house, jammed ourselves into a vanload, and headed for the grounds. It was a happy ride that grew even happier after we arrived and joined the foot-flow toward the center of the grounds. There were flags in abundance, bright silks of origin draped around necks and over shoulders. I recently attended a celebration in Monroe where the Swiss flag was omnipresent. It is natural to declare our heritage. When one of my relatives discovered the stranger in the carnitas line ahead of us hailed from his Central American hometown, the animation of their conversation—held in their mother tongue—was a pleasure to observe. I caught only a word here and there, but understood the moment fully.

We were there above all for the music and for two days there was much of it, all of it loud. When Prince Royce came out he was greeted with approval and confetti. I wanted to roll my eyes, but if I had a voice like that and abs like that and moves like that I'd sling long-stemmed roses too. What a lovely time I had dancing with my wife. I am resolutely and flat-footedly arrhythmic, but the key as I have come to learn is to dance the basic side-to-side bachata in close position. It will help if you are surrounded by thousands and a blazing light show. On the final evening it was Daddy Yankee, the reggaetón beat thudding through the foam ear plugs, the sound the equivalent of the faces turned toward the stage in joy, in that moment when the issue is not style or taste or but the love of shared human existence.

Back home in my quiet office, I read an interview of author Daniel José Older in which he said that in order to "write someone who isn't you" we must use "deep listening," then, "tell yourself a story based on that music." His comments derive from writing but speak to power and inclusivity. There are many ways to listen.

CHICK CHORES

Lately my keyboard has tended toward cloudy territory, so perhaps it is time to mention that out in our old granary at the moment there is a stock tank containing 25 peeping chicks. In fact if you've raised chicks you know they don't so much peep as whistle, the softest sort of whistle, concordant with the texture of their down. It is a soothing rather than a frantic sound.

The chicks arrived by mail, and are the charges of our younger daughter. She is hoping to gentle a few of them so they jump to her arms when grown. I have never had the patience to manage this. Our friend Billy has chickens that actually snuggle, but then again Billy once pawned a killer rooster off on me because Billy didn't have the heart to deal with the situation definitively. Three words, Billy, I said: *Coq au vin*. He winced and went back to cuddling his Ameraucana.

Oh but look, I've wandered off into grimness again. Let us return to those chicks, clustered under their heat lamp, nodding off and snoozing, sometimes with their winglets in the outrigger position and their chins flat on the sawdust.

They rouse unpredictably and skitter off to the feeder or the water trough, peck-pecking or gargling a dewdrop's worth of water. When it's time to refresh the feed and water they scatter like startled fish, but recover quickly and resume their former order as soon as we replace the screen over the tank. We weight the screen with four bricks before leaving, as there are cats and varmints about.

We have prepped our daughter with the idea that chick mortality is usually part of the deal, but so far—we are a week in, and I am stepping away from the keyboard now to rap the windowsill—every bird that arrived is still alive. One began to languish while I was away this week but my wife helped our daughter dip its beak in water several times over the course of a day and it seems to have recovered.

It is our daughter's responsibility to care for the chickens each morning before she begins her school lessons. So far she is operating with a pioneer spirit, although one suspects the task may lose its shine over time. Here in the early days there is enough newness and change to keep her interested. She is especially amazed at how quickly their wing feathers grow; like corn on a hot day, it almost seems possible to view the quills emerging from the sheath.

There is the hope that caring for these chicks will allow the child to understand responsibility; to the family, to critters dependent on us, to feeding others so she may feed herself. There is also the hope that whatever may come be it now or 80 years from now she holds the memory of what it is to cup the ephemeral weight of a living fuzz-ball in her hands. That no matter what dunderheaded human ugliness is pullulating all around us we must undertake gentle operations with hope for the future.

That her dad was prone to overthinking things, and sometimes it's just chicken chores.

POWER OUT

This morning deer were eating windfall apples in the yard and the valley below us was steeped in fog. Although the month has been trending unseasonably warm, the morning coolness is holding a fresh edge, and the trees are spotting up from green to various brilliants. We have yet to stoke our woodstove, but the suggestion has been raised. There is also the matter of filling the remaining empty cubic feet in the woodshed. We have an abundance of dry oak, but it has yet to be moved under tin. Check back with me in December to see if I'm pawing it out from under snow.

The chicks we took on a few weeks ago are growing apace. Shortly they will be too large for the stock tank they currently occupy. We'll ease them into an outside setup, allow them some earth-pecking time before it freezes up and goes bald beneath its snowcap. A few weeks of transition, then we'll transfer them to the main coop to ride out winter with the grownups. One hopes come spring they'll join the egg-laying brigade.

But we count on nothing. This morning we woke in the predawn to a house with no power. I'm still not sure what happened, as there was no storm or heavy winds, nor did my fire department pager go off (more than once when we've lost power, we've been dispatched to a car-versus-electrical pole accident five minutes later). While the kids got ready for cold breakfast by headlamp, I took the pickup and drove down the road to see if it was just us (we are at the tail end of a power line that passes through a lot of trees, so sometimes are the only ones without electricity). The neighbor's yard light was dark, as were those of the two other neighbors. I drove another mile to the house of a friend where our kids have showered and prepared for school during power losses in the past, and could see from the road that the juice was on there, so I headed back home. By the time I drove back into our yard the kitchen lights were burning. Power had been restored, as had the normal flow of the morning. During my little drive I'd had the radio on, and the news was of course dominated by the devastation of Puerto Rico, where they don't expect the electricity to return for months. I'm uncertain about the virtues of gauging our privileges based on someone else's devastation, but at the very least it seems worthy of consideration as one flicks the switch, specifically the idea that paying for something is not always equivalent to earning it.

In other words, get out there and move that firewood, son. Check those lantern batteries, recharge that flashlight. Fix the wheel on the chicken tractor, the one you're going to need next week if those chicks maintain their current feathery trajectory. And if you look out to see three deer eating red apples at sunrise as short-lived brightening leaves peek through a valley of fog, well stop and take a brain-picture of that for some future moment of unexpected darkness.

DENNY'S OK

The other day my wife called me and said I better go check on Denny. Denny is our neighbor, and a good one he is. He and his wife Linda are our chief chicken babysitters. We repay them in more eggs than they can use. Once Denny collected one of the wooden eggs we use to train the layers and foil the shell-peckers. Not recognizing it for what it was, Denny took it home and when it rolled off the countertop he lunged to catch it, then stood wide-eyed as it smacked the floor and didn't crack.

Ours is a lopsided relationship. Denny and Linda help us way more than we help them. They also feed our cats. And Denny is our informal security guard. He notices cars that don't belong. He catches trespassers and dead-end trash dumpers. When the garbage truck kept skipping our recycling stop up atop the hill, Denny let us put our bins down there on the main road by his mailbox. Once when I cleared a batch of steel posts from our garden by inadvertently peeling them out of the ground with our rear-mounted tractor tiller, Denny cut the twisted rebar out of the tiller tines with his cutting torch, chuckling the whole while. He also laughed that time I had to get him to come up and tow my minivan after I got it stuck in the woods while ferrying supplies to a deer blind.

I was at work in my office above the garage when my wife called. "I think you better come down here and check on Denny," she said. "His four-wheeler is parked oddly at the side of the road but I don't see him and he doesn't answer when I call." Denny's got a spot half-way up our hill where he backs his trailer to the edge of an embankment and dumps limbs and leaves and lawn clippings. When I got there his four-wheeler was at right angles to the road, backed so far off it his trailer was half-dangling over the edge. With trepida-tion I eased up to the four-wheeler and peeked over. As a first responder I've gone looking for people in these situations before, and more than once have found a body. Peeking around for that sort of thing is kinda like blowing up a balloon, not knowing when it will pop. I called Denny's name a couple of times. No answer.

I drove down the hill and hung a right into Denny's place. He came out of his shop, grinning shamefacedly and shaking his head. "I told Linda if I didn't get that thing outta there, someone would come huntin' me!" he said. He explained that he had somehow jammed the shift lever of the four-wheeler so it would only go in reverse, and in trying rock it loose he just kept backing up until he was trapped with the hind end hanging over the drop-off. Just to keep things square, I laughed at him.

But in truth I was deeply relieved. Denny and I aren't buddies. Our families don't hang out or party or socialize together. We mostly just honk and wave. But he and Linda are always there if we need something. The loveliness of this sort of neighborliness is even sweeter because it doesn't depend on much else beyond garden-variety civility. After I helped Denny tow the four-wheeler back down the hill and into his shop we went our separate ways for the rest of the day, but as I settled back into my work up the hill it was good to know he was OK down there. A neighbor, neighborly as need be.

MOVE THE CHICKS

The two dozen chicks had outgrown the stock tank and thus had to be moved. We couldn't relocate them directly into the main coop, as the older hens are prone to peck rather than mother. So I headed down to the pole barn to resurrect the bomb crate. We call it the bomb crate because it's a three-foot tall rectangular plywood cube on wheels, built more to keep varmints out than chickens in. We usually use it for the meat chickens, as they are not nimble and do not roost. It is esthetically dubious (one of the plywood sheets had a prior life as a billboard and still bears advertising for a commercial real estate salesman) but dead solid, and was built for barter by our friend Todd. I don't recall the exact terms but the transaction included a used van featuring wall-switch wipers and a sketchy transmission.

One of the bomb crate tires was flat and I had to do some carpentry touch-up (six misused drywall screws later, we were good to go). There was also a squeaky axle situation, easily remedied with a spritz of my favorite cologne, WD-40. I finished up by repositioning a door hook and re-stapling the loose plastic feed sack that keeps the autumn wind out, then rolled the whole deal into place adjacent to the grownup chicken run.

There were young cousins visiting from the city, so we had a lot of help. While they prepped the crate with fresh shavings, I set up a little pen. Then, handful by fluffy handful, we began the transfer. There was a lot of nervous peeping, but most of the birds acclimated quickly. They pecked vigorously at their first greens, exploding in gangly leaps and short-arc flutter flights to celebrate the width and breadth of their new world. And yet, even in the moment there is the unease of seeing those delicate creatures right out in the open. Knowing from experience we cannot protect them from every little thing. How unlikely it is that they will all make it. How I have come out to find a dozen chickens laid out dead in a row, the work of a weasel poaching the roost. How quickly the hawk strikes. How sometimes you just find one dead at dawn. And yet you cannot keep them in that stock tank.

We clustered around the pen. The air was cool, the sky was blue, the maple leaves overhead colored and lit by sun. That barrel-thick maple trunk was the circumference of my arm when my wife and I were wed beneath it. Our waist-high flower girl that day is now our teenager, towering over me, just months from emancipation and being set loose in the world. The misty eyes and metaphor require no further description.

One of my nieces—not even born when we bought this farm—stayed with the birds long after everyone else returned to the house. I kept an eye on her as I did some miscellaneous chores, then just sat to watch as she cuddled and cooed at the chicks, gently introducing the hesitant ones to their new feed and water stations. When her mother came for her, the little girl promised the chicks she would return.

Now I am typing this final line near midnight. From here I

can see the yellow warmth of the heat light seeping out a crack in the crate, the birds for now safe within, the children asleep in their beds, the days coming one at a time.

APPLE WASPS

The apple was crawling with wasps. The fruit was half-rotted on the branch, and the wasps were worming well in beneath the peel. There were easily twenty-five of them, swarming the flesh in a crawly, flexing, burrowing horde. The weather was cool enough that I could get right in there for a look without any of them taking flight or stinging my dumb face. Even were it warmer there was the sense that they were far too consumed with feeding their sugar buzz to buzz in anger.

It's been a waspy season. Perhaps no more or less than other years; I'm not dialed in to the trends. I do know that this fall the siding was coated with them and this summer I got stung on my bald head when I disturbed one of those small inverted-mushroom nests dangling from a corner of the garage door. It happened while the rest of the family was loaded up and waiting in the van, so they had a wide wind-shield view of my head-slapping dance routine. It was impro-vised on the fly but got rave reviews. Extra points were awarded for my ability to pummel my own cranium while simultaneously executing 360-degree pirouettes in a bouncing crouch reminiscent of a traditional whirling

Russian afflicted with iffy hips. Some things must be witnessed live to be appreciated. By the time we got to the end of the driveway the knot on my temple was such that I could no longer wear my hat. Later I cleaned out all the tiny nests I could find, but just this week, thirty feet up in in the maple tree overhanging the driveway, I spied a paper nest big as a fat raccoon.

So: there are a lot of wasps. That's my official take. Please notify the proper national Hymenoptra census representatives.

The mass of apple-eating wasps was one of those attractive-repulsive sights from which you cannot avert your eyes. Of course it's an utterly natural tableau, but then so is a turkey vulture hooking its beak into a three-days-dead deer alongside some road in July. It is a natural and wonderful sight, but it would not have been out of place in a 1990s Nine Inch Nails video. I called the kids over for a look and posted a video on social media, as that is what we do with all contemporary wonderments and minutiae.

Hits and likes are fine, but I had come to the apple tree in the first place to get an apple. I reached into the boughs and plucked a waspless one. It was a bird-pecked, pitted, and imperfect fruit, but firm with here and there some unsullied patches of skin. I rotated to one of these and bit. The chunk came away crisply, with a juicy crack and snap commensurate to the autumn air. The taste was clean and sweet. I stood beneath the blazing yellow leaves, feasting with hornets.

WEAPONS OF MASS DESTRUCTION

There currently resides upon my desk a Certificate of Completion declaring that I have checked all the boxes necessary to satisfy the standards set forth by my compulsory biannual refresher course in Weapons of Mass Destruction.

Next to the electric bill, that's a showstopper.

This does not mean that if you find a nuclear warhead in your flower garden you should call me. My training is broad and basic, and I share it with all first responders in the state, including the neighbors beside whom I am privileged to serve on those occasions when I am home to answer the page. In many cases of mass hazard we are taught to back off and call someone more qualified. While it is critical that we train to run toward trouble, it is equally critical that we not be devoured by the trouble before we can supply succor. "Secure the scene" is our foremost mantra.

Sounds simple until you sit in a fire hall conference room and review the multitude of ways the human race has devised to extinguish itself. It is even more sobering to realize that even as we add new means to the list someone is busying themselves with an angle not yet plied. As the video narrator ticks off a history of atrocities you feel simultaneously vulnerable and just happy to be here. You may possibly stop on the way home for an unhealthy gas station doughnut if only to experience the simple joy of walking freely between your fellow citizens, most of whom live oblivious to all these things afoot. I can tell you it also leads to sitting in the van outside the garage staring at the house, wondering how much of this you should share with your family. (The class in question also included a bracing review of our collective firsthand experience with rural pharmaceuticals.)

I've never been taken with the idea of destiny. That things happen because they were destined to happen. Many disagree for many reasons, and I'm not looking to tussle over it. But I'd prefer to think that if I'm knocked flat by a pipe bomb, it was not a higher plan, it was a most specific and nefarious plan. That if I am overtaken by the ammonia plume, I shoulda checked the wind, or I just didn't see it coming, or I got caught up in trying to do some good.

I dunno. I despair over all the division. Historically speaking, I worry it's worse than we think. This is hardly an original observation, and I'll do no good whining. Plus I got no zippy solutions. But as I fish that certificate out from amongst the desk-litter in order to turn it in down at the station, I am certain of this: for all the horror inherent in its existence, I prefer the facts, matter-of-fact. Then to get on with the business of the day-to-day, until called to do otherwise.

CHICKEN WATER HEATER

Against the advice of one of my most revered and trusted mentors, the late Gene Logsdon, we have ordered a heated poultry waterer.

I have been down this road before, and it didn't end well. Early in our poultry-raising days, I bought an over-priced, over-powered heating coil to place beneath the galvanized chicken waterer over the winter season. I did this with some reservation, as amateur heating solutions are one of the leading causes of chicken coop fires, and I am not kidding. But one grows so weary of dealing with buckets of ice, and on some of your subzero stretches the water goes solid before the chickens get their recommended daily allowance. I rigged the element beneath and between some bricks so the water would be directly above it.

It kinda worked. Trouble is, once the eggs are laid, you have a coopful of bored winterbound chickens free to devote every second of their existence to their favorite hobby: cramming all available crevices with wood chips, feathers, and chaff—then frosting the whole works with a hearty encrustation of poop. Within days the heating element was—in every sense—a hot mess.

The topper though, came the freezing morning I discovered they had managed to unplug the thing. I plugged it back in and finished the feeding chores. Before exiting the coop, I checked to be sure the element was heating. What I did was, I just reached under there and grabbed it. It was one of those deals where you hear the sizzle before the *Yeowch!* makes the journey. *Idiot!* I said. OK, actually I said something worse. And then I stuffed my hand in the snow and held it there a while as I considered my knuckleheaditude. From within the coop came the sound of chickens snickering.

In his book "The Contrary Farmer," Gene Logsdon recommended against wasting time and money futzing with heaters and rather using old bleach bottles or detergent bottles—something made of flexible plastic. When they freeze, he wrote, simply knock the ice out and put in fresh water. After a winter of hassling with that heating element, I switched to Gene's method, using rubber feeding pans. Flip it, stomp it, refill it. Simple.

But now a new heated waterer has been invented. One that stands above all the mess and is designed so that chickens can't roost on it. I have been tempted off the path of utility by the allure of smooth surfaces, thermostat technology, and no ice-stomping. The package is on its way, and so is the first snow. We'll see. If it works as advertised I worry my character will weaken with the ease of it.

Conversely, over there across the yard are forty-or-so chickens about to hole up for the winter with no hobbies save one: How to frustrate the humans. Individually they are pea-brains; in a flock they are MIT with multi-tool beaks.

Gene Logsdon has been gone just over a year now, and here I am betraying his legacy. That said, knowing him as I did, nothing would tickle his funny bone more than me getting burnt. Again.

HALLOWEEN

Come Halloween one of my children composed a costume requiring eyeglasses. She approached me in my work room over the garage and asked if I could spare a pair, which in fact I could, as I buy "cheaters" in bulk and distribute them generally and vastly around the acreage. They are cheap in terms of both dollars and quality, and therefore when she asked if I could pop the lenses out to prevent her getting blurry headaches, I could, and easily did.

At risk of incurring disfavor I will admit I have lost the Halloween buzz. The last time I really got into it was about eight years ago when I went to the family party dressed as the International Harvester logo, an esoteric choice but much appreciated in the environs of my raising. I had to turn sideways to fit my "H" through the door, and before eating sloppy joes had to remove the dot from the "i" as it was a spray-painted box enclosing my cranium.

Nowadays I mostly just dig a wig and a witch hat out of the orange plastic tubs containing our All Hallow's Eve accouterments and call it good. Mainly I do it for the children. And then they do things for me, like deviate from the high-density trick-or-treat route in town in order to drop in on our octogenarian neighbor Tom. My ulterior motive here was to get a picture of him with my children, one of them taller than he now, and possibly making her final Halloween stop.

I understand their desire to get to town, where more houses are lit than not, and the pickings are rich. Especially at the taverns, where they tend to hand out big honking candy bars. Among my favorite father memories I count the times I trailed down the sidewalk with all the other parents as we sent our costumed tiny tots one after the other into the saloons. There is a certain roughneck looseness to small town life that—in a world of antiseptic wipes and nice clean soccer shorts—can be exhilarating.

Up north at my parents farm, where the address is remote and there are few doors to knock upon, we again this year set up a self-contained "scary walk" in which the kids trailed from barn to shed and so on, and were offered treats by vaguely familiar ghouls. "I know it's you, Uncle John!" they say, their high-pitched giggles betraying uncertainty none-theless. I myself spent quite a lot of time shivering in the milk house before they finally arrived. I scared them by rattling the lids on the bulk tank.

Now the costumes are packed in the tubs again. The austere, bony part of autumn is here, and there have been a couple of decent snows. My wife asked that I replace the screen door on the porch with the solid wooden one. I did it right away, for a change. I had a little struggle getting the screws and hinges lined up. Grabbed a pair of those cheap reading glasses off the kitchen counter but they didn't help much, and it was only after much squinting and head-tipping that I got the thing hung. Wore those glasses a good fifteen minutes before I took them off and realized they didn't have any lenses in them.

NO CHICKENS ON BOOK TOUR

Yesterday I spent the morning rearranging the chicken fencing. We are introducing a flock of young ones to a flock of older ones. This transition is not always harmonious. In fact, we have segregated the rooster for bad behavior before he has a chance to exhibit any. The phrase "pecking order" is not entirely benign. Also, the younger birds must learn to navigate an enclosed ramp leading into the "grownup" coop. This will require rewiring their brains over the course of a few days and may require actual trails of bread crumbs. It will certainly require patience, and I won't be there for any of it, as once I got the fencing re-set, I lit out on a nine-day book tour.

The book I am out touting is about a dead French philosopher. This is clearly a coup of target marketing, as you have to believe the world is thirsting for my take on the musings of a 16th-century essayist, when in fact I can't even properly pronounce his name. (Michel de Montaigne, which when delivered in the proper French is as mellifluous as soft summer breeze blown across soft summer cheese; delivered by me it sounds like, Yah, I like them deep-fried curds.)

Montaigne lived in a castle in the country so most likely had some chickens around the place, but as he was not only a philosopher but a nobleman likely did not have to clean the coop himself. He certainly didn't have to stand bald in the bitter November wind and rig up a temporary poultry chute made of lath, chicken wire, orange plastic construction fence, steel rebar, and an abundance of bungee cords.

But I protest too much, because I am now in a hotel room in Minneapolis, far from my chicken responsibilities. (Although—and I am not making this up—I just noticed some evidence of yesterday morning's chores has accompanied me, specifically something that just came off my boot heel and is now on the carpet. Happily, it was dry and easily disposed of.)

Out of respect to those holding down the fort, I just checked in with my wife on the state of things. Turns out she and our younger daughter spent the waning daylight hour coaxing the young chickens into the enclosed ramp, then gently levering and plunger-ing them up the incline using sticks and dried weed plumes. There were some escapees and stowaways and my wife wound up crawling around in the sawdust, and it was dark and bitterly cold by the time they finished. My wife says this morning about 17% of the chickens figured out how to come down the ramp, so based on the poultry learning curve we're on track for total compliance come Christmas.

I have some ideas on how I might speed up the process, but I kept my mouth shut. There is a line in this book I'm out here promoting, and I'll close with it: During a recent interview with a women's magazine, a traveling writer was asked if there was anything special he did for his wife when he was away from home, and I replied, yes, I don't call her and tell her how to run things.

TURKEY DAYS

If the center has held, the earth has not spun off its axis, and I have maintained a detectable pulse, you will be reading this in the tryptophanic wake of Thanksgiving. I preface the sentence as I do because I have never grown completely comfortable composing lines that assume the future, filled with uncertainty as life is (just ask the turkey). It also occurs to me that certain research-based scolds have taken to suggesting that there really isn't enough tryptophan in that turkey to make you sleepy and in fact your heavy lids are probably predicated more on exceeding the maximum recommended dosage of mashed potatoes and gravy than anything, but I didn't go to the trouble of learning to spell tryptophan only to give up that easily.

My grandfather used to cook the Thanksgiving turkey (or perhaps it was the Christmas turkey?) in a red Weber grill outside the garage of his red brick split-level. We were farm kids from a large family that never grilled, so the scent of the briquettes was exotic, so different than the scent of the slab pile bonfire, or the burn barrel. The turkey as I recall it was smokily delicious and Grandpa sliced it up with an electric knife that was also a thing of wonder. How magical the memory power that allows a meal to be eaten again, savored a second time. To summon the muffled buzz of the blade passing through the white meat, to see each slice curling into place on the plate. To see Grandpa—gone decades now—smiling, trim, and nimble, dressed in slacks and a golf shirt, an outfit also exotic to us hand-me-down farm jean kids.

As I've grown older I find myself simultaneously cherishing these sorts of Instamatic memories (I see them in the super-saturated colors of snapshots taken with a rotating flashcube) while trying not to dive into them over-frequently. We must gird ourselves for the present, deal with the wolf at the door or the Chihuahua nipping at our heels, not disappear mooning into the past, where after all nothing can be fixed.

I say this as I anticipate a week spent mostly in the woods (again, in this typing time warp I am telling you after I am out of the woods I am looking forward to going into the woods) during which—as I have been spending this week in the woods every year for 40 years now—I know from prior experience I will spend the bulk of my time in reflection (when not napping in the open air, an underappreciated art), much of which reflection will leave me realizing I am coming up short in the present.

That's okay. To sit in the cold woods feeling teensy and inadequate is—I always find—a necessary re-set. There is an astringent effect, a stripping away of the day-to-day hoo-hah we leverage to help us ignore the fact that we are but little critters scurrying around a giant rock. When I come out of the woods I always feel less afflicted with nonsense. I also feel I have rediscovered hunger. True hunger. Good news being, there is still turkey in the fridge, enough for a thick sandwich, the exact sort of fortification required to take on the silly wobbly world again, although perhaps first a nap.

SLEEPY

This past week—as threatened last week—I stole a fine nap on a bed of shed pine needles. There are those who would say I was letting my guard down, and of course I was. What greater privilege could there be in this dangerous world than to not only lower your guard but abandon it to the open sky. Per the neighbor's game cameras, there are many bears in my sleep zone, but by this time of year they too are napping, so I felt good about my chances, waking-up-wise. I was deer hunting, so it could be argued that a snooze rendered me insubordinate in my duties as an apex predator but I've never been top-flight in that role anyway.

The thing was, I had been out and about since pre-dawn. At noon, I returned to the house and had perhaps a bit too much for lunch. Then, after walking way out back I hunkered down under a young thick-boughed white pine, beneath which was laid the burnt orange carpet. It happened at this moment that the afternoon sun was cutting through the atmosphere in a way that toasted my face even as the air I breathed remained icy. It is good to breathe cold air when you are warm. I stretched out on my back then, if only to aid digestion. The land was at an incline of such that my feet were just a touch lower than my head, and in short order I was asleep.

When I awoke I felt deeply refreshed, the way we do when the brain cycles solidly through the necessary reset but has not shut down to the point of sluggishness. People smarter than I can explain the electro-cellular specifics, but I know it when I feel it. I didn't move right away, rather stayed flat, staring through gaps in the white pine branches to the gray sky above, re-tuning myself to my surroundings by simply listening. Second thing I heard after the wind was wild turkeys calling yelp and purr—the language of keeping in touch. I eased my head up slowly and there they were, arranged along the edge of the ice-skimmed pond forty yards downhill. They were pecking at the ice, punching little holes from which they dipped water. I watched them for a long time. At one point there were a full dozen in view.

After the last of them slipped quietly into the weeds and brown brush, I raised myself to a sitting position and resumed my predator role. It was easy work, as nothing much happened. I just sat until the sun went down and I heard the turkeys go branch-smashingly to their roosts. Roosting turkeys have all the natural subtlety of airborne weed-whack-ers. By the time I got home it was good and dark. I closed up the chicken coop and fed the cats. When I stepped into the kitchen I was surprised to see it was just past 5 p.m. It seemed so much later. The rest of the family was away on a trip (they like to free me up for my apex predator duties), so I ate dinner alone. I had all intentions of getting some work done then, but the long open-air day had taken its lovely toll, and I retired early. My last conscious thought was of the pine tree overhead, and turkeys, and bears, and soon all of us asleep.

SKIFF SNOW

The ground is windswept and hard, overlain with a skiff of snow. When I open the chicken coop door the birds spill cackling forth and attack the feed pails as they do on any given day, but when I look across the yard an hour later they have retreated back within. I guess the ol' scratch-and-peck loses its zip when your beak is scraping solid sod.

I have always enjoyed the word "skiff" as it pertains to precipitation. Surely it is more widely recognized as the term for a small boat, but in the frozen parts of the Midwest we also deploy it to describe thin windrows of snow that create their own visual wind chill. Meaning, whereas a "blanket" of snow conveys a coziness that adds ten imaginary mind degrees to the landscape, an anemic snow cover cut with exposed strips of frozen dirt renders the face of the earth more bitter than the thermometer might register.

The chickens aren't especially interested in the distinction. They don't care to hang out and peck around on a skiff, but neither do they like the deep stuff. In fairness to the poultry, they aren't really outfitted for snowshoeing. We still open their door on winter days when it's not below zero, and they pop out to test the air, maybe huddle on the bare patch under the coop if the sun is hitting just right, but then it's right back inside to the wood shavings and heated water bucket. I assume they cannot anticipate spring and are therefore not impatient for it. It could be argued that for all their clucking, chickens are good at equanimity. For all I know they're in there playing canasta.

For us humans, the upside of a "skiff" is that our tasks are more easily completed. I can trek out to do those chicken chores without first shoveling a pathway. The woodshed is an easy walk rather than a shin-deep slog. And I have so far avoided mounting the snowplow. Also—and this is not inconsequential—your "skiff" snow means no whining about shoveling the sidewalk from the younger set. In that sense, the threadbare blanket means peace on earth.

But: This week we'll go out back, to a stand of spruce just beyond the old hog pen, and cut ourselves a Christmas tree. It'd sure be nice to drag it back over snow rather than across frozen mud-nubs. We'll also weave coils of blue and white lights around the deck railing, and they always look cheerier when amplified by mounds of white—even if those mounds were pushed in place by whiny children slumping over their shovels.

In short, I am pulling for a white Christmas. This is not an especially original sentiment, but our deepest comforts are well-worn. If, come that day, I am warm and well-fed in the company of family, it will be sufficient, snow or no, but I hope for snow. The chickens are indifferent, and have neither hopes nor plans. Merry Christmas. Happy Holidays. Cluck-ety-cluck.

OLD YEAR'S RESOLUTIONS

Just before Christmas I had a colonoscopy, which seems an appropriate conclusion to the year passed. The fact that I elected to undergo the procedure without anesthesia was my own fault and yields a tale for another time (did you know you can sweat green?), but I feel as if the session left me better prepared for whatever the new year may deliver. And if not prepared, calibrated.

I understand this may not be the specific festive imagery you had in mind when you settled in for a good read with your morning coffee, but life is a series of unwarranted surprises, the days not so much unfolding as replicating in the manner of linoleum mold. There are blooms, but they are not always fragrant.

In this our season of self-assessment and self-improvement I don't know what to tell you. Here compiled in no particular order, is all I've got:

1. If you are entering into a business arrangement with someone who repeatedly and grandly announces, "money is no object," by all means get paid up front.

2. If they say they will, they might.

3. I prefer "grey" over "gray" but spellcheck shames me over this, as do underpaid copyeditors.

4. The reason that air compressor was on sale and cheaper than all the others was because none of the attachments were included. Not the hose, not the chuck, not the coupler, not the gauge. Pretty picture of all those items on the box, though. So pretty you might overlook the fine print.

5. If you're trying to pull up one of those step-in fence posts and it just won't budge, no matter how hard you grunt and heave, umm, check to make sure you're not standing on the step-in.

6. You really can't call yourself a farmer unless you've got at least one purple fingernail.

7. If you emanate an invisible force field that prevents the functioning of "automatic" soap dispensers, faucets, and paper towel machines, you are not alone. I stand there flapping my hands like I'm conducting Beethoven's Fifth and get not so much as a drip.

8. The tape measure blade will always slip off the end of the 2×4 when you don't want it to, but clings tight when you try to shake it loose. Despite all the formulas, physics remain a mystery. In this specific case, someone needs to do a little more research on the blood pressure coefficient.

9. The secret to happiness? The cultivation of friends, neighbors, and loved ones to whom #2 does not apply.

In conclusion, I realize some of you with English degrees or a tendency toward postmodern supracontextual meta-analysis or who are my Mom may be reading between the lines and assigning undue significance to certain items as evidence of undisclosed inner turmoil. In fact these are just the things that came to mind with my coffee or popped up when I searched my own blog. Before I left the clinic last week I was told my colon looked good, which is quite a lesson in the contrast between the objective and the aesthetic. And so, ho-ho, off we go.

THANK YOU STAMP

Mom taught me to write thank you notes, and so I try to do. I admit I have fallen behind in recent years. In part this is good news: how fortunate I am to be unable to fairly thank everyone who does me a good turn, a kindness, or delivers my pocket notebook to the high school office after finding it in the bleachers the morning after my daughter's final volleyball game.

Right this very moment there is a to-thank list as long as my forearm taped to my desk. Many of these are related to a recent book tour. I feel a thank you is especially important in this instance since the visits were brief but the hosts' preparations were long. Less professionally I only recently mailed a thank-you to my cousin for hosting us in Nashville last summer. We are scheduled for a return visit soon and I feared the thank you note and we might arrive simultaneously.

I scribble many of my thank-you notes on postcards left over from various book promotions. Economic self-interest is in play (recouped printing costs, cheaper stamps, and I might accidentally sell a book), but I solemnly swear the sentiment in the scribble is as authentic as the signature.

When a postcard won't do, or might come off as crass, I go first class. During a book tour several years ago, I was kindly gifted stationery embossed with my name. I found this most authorial, and enjoy dashing off notes thereupon with a fountain pen, as if I were Mark Twain's penmanship-impaired stepchild. Trouble is, this stationery is square and of a dimension that, if folded, slops around in a standard envelope most inartistically. Because aesthetics are my part-time thing, I went online and to extra expense obtaining envelopes that were not only the dimension of the stationery but conveyed a rough-hewn artfulness. In short, they are the color and texture of a feed mill gunny sack.

How I loved jotting my thanks then slipping the paper unfolded into the envelope to be stamped and sent. How sweet it was to imagine the words drawn uncreased from within to warm a deserving heart. How shamed I was last week when I sent one to a local artistic collaborator whose husband happens to be both a friend of mine and a former post office employee, which is to say he didn't mind informing me that his wife's card arrived postage due and envelopes that size require another twenty-one cents.

This means that over the course of a few years my thank you notes have cost their recipients a collective 117 dollars, minimum. My embarrassment is matched only by my admiration for the character and courteousness of these folks in that only now has someone raised a stink, and even that in the name of friendship.

The extra stamps are now on hand. My thanks will no longer arrive by invoice, and my commitment to the gracious habit is renewed. The world is speedy, vituperous, and rude; a handwritten word of gratitude seems a sweet comma between it all.

ABOVE ZERO

If the app on my phone is correct, by the time you read this conditions will have ascended to that tropical zone known around these parts as "above zero," a meteorological Shangri-La compared to the past week in which the mercury—digital and analog—has operated in bathyscaphe range, plumbing a sustained negative double digits dive. Chicken chores alone can cost you an earlobe.

On one of the coldest days this week, I called my neighbor Tom to check in on how he was doing down-valley. Fine, he said, in part because he recalled his family enduring a stretch of 39 or 40 consecutive subzero days in 1932 or 1936. Both of those "or's" are mine, by the way. Tom was firm and certain on both counts, but I can't remember which, bottom line being his 88-year-old long-term memory whomps my 53-year-old short-term capacity. Plus I've never been good with numbers. And lately my head has been frozen a lot.

Point is, what Tom was doing there was elucidating the difference between a cold snap and a cold streak. He didn't actually say, "Toughen up there, Sparky," but it was implied. And back then being the 1930s young Tom's family wouldn't have had access to the cheats I employ, among them self-warming chicken waterers, off-peak electric thermal storage (a plugged-in box of bricks, basically), and pan heaters.

My teenaged daughter received her introduction to this latter marvel when I sent her off to her weekend job last Friday with a pan heater nestled inside its own coiled extension cord within her car trunk. She was just tickled. I showed her where the oil pan was, I showed her how the magnets fix the heater to the bottom of the oil pan, and I told her if you grab it anywhere other than by the handle that thing will scorch your fingerprints right off, never mind how I know.

Ever vigilant for the teachable moment and fearing that she might take the easy and warm way out, I also explained that not only do we attach the pan heater so the car will start more easily, but also because cold-cranking a car engine at fifteen below will cost you in maintenance fees down the road. She is a delightful and responsible young woman of whom I am most proud; nonetheless in her eyes I saw a benign vacancy like she believed me but only believed me in the way I believed my parents until I really did start paying for my own radiator hoses. It's like telling someone from Florida the difference between ten above and ten below. Until it bites them in the face, they can only nod in ignorance.

Three days, the phone says, and then it will be warm again. Threatening the upper 20s, and then, on a distant Wednesday, two degrees above your standard freezing point. I'll uncoop the chickens. I'll watch water fall from the eaves in liquid form. I'll stir up some lemonade and air up the beach ball. And thirty-five years from now, should I be allowed the gift of longevity and the forgetfulness of others, I will tell the story of that stretch in 2017 when it was thirty below for forty days straight and I only survived by sitting on a pan heater.

REFREEZE

Last week I described a spate of relief unleashed by the mercury pushing above zero after a sustained run of negative digits. Naturally, by the time the column hit print our nose hairs were froze again. As if I don't give people enough reason to question my intelligence as it is. Such are the latent dangers of early deadlines.

Today's cold blew in after two days of melt and an unseasonable fog. Coming home from play rehearsal last night I nearly stuffed my rig in the ditch on that curve just down from our neighbor Tom's place. The fog had settled and was skinning into ice. The rest of the way home I proceeded at half the speed, my eyes twice as wide.

By morning it had all gone to sleet and the schools were closed. By breakfast the flakes were falling thickly. We bolstered the firewood reserves and brought all the feeders back inside the chicken coop and gave the birds an extra taste of corn. Then the kids did their homework, I did mine, and my wife worked on the taxes. Cozy, everyone about their business.

Late in the afternoon the snow thinned out, the wind picked up, and the mercury was in steep decline. We bundled into our coats and snow pants and set out for the back forty on cross-country skis. This sort of thing would never happen were it not for my wife, who has some ideas about fresh air, fitness, and family.

We journeyed together for the most part. Took our turns breaking trail. Then at the turnaround point my wife and the teenager began to pull away. The ten year old and I compounded our lagging by stopping to watch a coyote sneaking off through the sumac. And then four deer traversing a cross-valley hillside. We concocted a story about a princess who couldn't get the stationery store to spell her name right. Speed isn't everything.

When we turned for home we were in the teeth of the wind. Ten minutes later the youngster said she could no longer feel her thumbs. The way she spoke it was clear she also couldn't feel her lips. Standing windbreak, I enveloped her cold hands in my warm ones, then gave her my facemask. By the time we strode into the yard she was sufficiently re-warmed to join her mother on the toboggan for a few runs down past the pole barn.

Meanwhile, the teenager asked me to teach her to run the snow plow, an adventure of an entirely different sort. Our first pass out the driveway we met up with a neighbor with whom there had been a recent misunderstanding involving the etiquette of deer hunting. It was time to talk it out and we did, and it was awkward at first and now it's not anymore. My daughter watched from a distance and I hope snowplowing isn't the only thing she learned today.

Finally we reconvened in the woodstove-warm house. Supper was especially good, what with all the fresh air preceding. After the kids were in bed I checked my phone for the weather. Five degrees and falling. Winds out of the north, pushing double figures. I swiped to the news. Some shiftless politician, speaking drool. I placed the phone facedown, fed the fire, and listened to the wind blow.

OLD SCHOOL

Today I walked the halls of my old university on my way to a college radio station studio where I was interviewed about the local music "scene." This implies I am a red-hot insider, but in truth I was being imported more as a dean of history, or—let's cut to the chase—the very personification of a golden oldie.

The physical layout of the campus has changed dramatically since I attended. (Just now it occurs to me the same could be said regarding my own physical layout.) Still, the familiar bones of the surroundings triggered the usual blend of nostalgia, recognition, and head-shaking as I marveled at the manifest passage of time. I also had to suppress the urge to accost random students and yell things like "RIGHT HERE? THERE USED TO BE A PHONE BOOTH!" or "WHO MOVED THE LIBRARY?!?!" or simply, "MIMEOGRAPHS!"

The student who faced me across microphones appeared to have been freshly excused from junior high. I don't mean to be insulting, or to question his status as a scholar, I'm just saying there's nothing like peering at youth over your reading glasses to make you feel immediately geriatric.

Early in the interview I mentioned that this self-same university radio station had been a real ear-opener for me back in the day. I arrived in the big city a country boy familiar with little more than poppy Top 40. Thus I still clearly recall the night I accidentally tuned down the dial and heard a tongue-tied communications major broadcasting a song by an obscure band out of Athens, Georgia, that went by the name R.E.M. It was also on these airwaves that I first heard a song called "Pride (In the Name of Love)" by some up-and-comers named U2. In both instances my definition of "good" music wandered off the centerline to tastes I still trace.

"Oh, I bet it was on this album," the interviewer said, jumping up to retrieve a CD case from the shelf when I mentioned the R.E.M. tune. "It's been here *forever!*" He was so eager to please; it was with heavy heart I informed him that the CD he held was released in 1991...seven albums after the one I had referenced, and four years after I had graduated from college. The expression on his face suggested he very badly wanted to ask me what it was like plowing with oxen.

Music or otherwise, I'm always skeptical of the concept of a "scene." Seems to me once you've identified it, the deterioration has already set in. That's not as grumpy as it sounds. The cracks create space for new shoots. Some rise in the form of youthful disc jockeys in an age when "disc" has as much relevance as "wax cylinder." Perhaps it is a product of our contemporary political slaw, but I for one welcome the infiltrations of youth, what with their energy and hope and general lack of poisonous fear.

On the walk back to my car I passed through the oldest building on the grounds. When my father attended, that building *was* the university. One day on his way to class Dad got caught up in a human traffic jam when a campaigning John F. Kennedy entered the hallway. Pressed against the wall, Dad found himself at the end of an impromptu receiving line. Kennedy worked his way down the line, shaking every hand offered, only to peel off just before he reached my father. Dad always chuckled in the telling of it. It occurred to me as I drove away that history is a handful of echoes.

READING REMINISCENCE

The other evening my wife offered to share aloud a passage from the book she was reading. I grudgingly agreed, as I have never enjoyed being read to as an adult. If someone says, "Hey, listen to this," and rattles a newspaper, or is holding a book, or wielding an e-reader, I tense up and want to run the other way. It's a confounding conundrum, as I loved being read to as a child, but for some reason, as a grownup my first instinct is to grit my teeth. I am ashamed of this because I know many couples who love reading to each other, and assume my hang-up is symptomatic of selfishness, egotism, impatience, and any number of other traits all traceable to rank narcissism. My wife is well aware of this predilection, and thus rarely attempts to share. Shame on me, because she reads regularly and widely.

And so, in the interest of self-improvement as a means of alleviating self-loathing, I turned to my wife and said, "Yes, please." Then I put my head back and closed my eyes and she read the opening sentences of Laurie Lee's *Cider With Rosie*, a memoir of the author's childhood in rural England. I adapted a meditative pose, determined to overcome my dumb stubbornness. By the second sentence I found myself enchanted.

This reading took place at bedtime, and I drifted off feeling a nostalgic tug from a place I'd never been. Consequently, the next morning, during chicken chores, I contemplated the fact that somewhere in my late forties, I stopped looking at old photographs. Previously I loved noodling through vintage International Harvester refrigerator advertisements, old yearbooks, or tubs of family albums. The sense of transport, of time-travel, of cheating back to the past, was tantalizing and palliative. Tantalizing because there arises an actual physical sensation one is playing hooky on the hectic hairy present; palliative because you're able to ignore—if not postpone—the unrelenting encroachments of the future.

But something over the past handful of years has dulled my appetite for reminiscence. In part I suspect this is due to reminiscence's debt to sentimental nostalgia, which is not only useless in the face of the world's suffering, it is often used to obscure and perpetuate it. Every time we pine for "the good old days," we ignore the underside of history's iceberg.

The passage of time has also left me less and less able to endure the sweet sadness referred to by the Portuguese as saudade. In my youth saudade made me feel like a noble poetic loner. These days it just warps into worries about health insurance deductibles and the kid's earache.

Jeepers, I've wandered off into the weeds. The point is, as my wife began reading that book to me I was immediately drawn into a departed English countryside setting I'd never known, and yet the emotional resonance was immediate and clearly related to my own childhood in an American countryside. Eyes closed, I felt I was in a childlike, mystic place. Reflecting on this the following morning while pouring chicken feed I decided that for all its unreliability, reminiscence is worth revisiting as a simple mind vacation. Moderation and titration are key. The occasional backward gaze, then look to the future.

As for the present? Sit still, son, and allow yourself to be read to.

WIN THE DAY

Today I spoke to a gymnasium filled with high schoolers. I was charged with encouraging them to "win the day" and ask themselves, "what's your plan?"

Wowza. Talk about underqualified.

Let me be clear: I took the charge to heart, and spoke from same. I'm always baffled by what teenaged ears might hear when an unknown bald dad speaks, and I try to defuse things right out of the gate by making it clear I'm not there to convince the youngsters I'm hip and cool. I was hip for about a week in 1989 and cool for five minutes in 1994, but that was it and certainly never both at the same time. The bald dad line usually gets a muted little chuckle and everything goes better after that. (As both a father and a public speaker, I can tell you that on the laughter equivalency scale, a muted chuckle from a teenager equates to a rip-roaring bar-buddy guffaw; you take what you can get.)

Anyways, as we say (yep, outsiders, it's plural on purpose), I then launched into a description of my "career path," which in fact is a guidance counselor's worst nightmare and is more accurately expressed when "career" and "path" are sent to separate rooms and allowed their own scare quotes.

Kids, I really didn't know what I was doing. Grew up a farm boy, logging in the winters, cutting hay in the summer, and running an all-season pitchfork. Put myself through nursing school by working as a cowboy in Wyoming and a roller-skating Snoopy in Wisconsin. Got out of the cowboy business because I was scared of horses, which is, as they say, inimical to the endeavor. Got out of the roller-skating Snoopy business because, well, a lot of reasons, but mainly, Have you ever smelled the inside of a Snoopy suit?

By then I had a nursing degree. As employability goes, that's the wisest move I've ever made. Freed me up to wander off that path and off a series of cliffs with that nursing license tucked in my back pocket like a parachute. Haven't worked as a nurse for nearly 30 years now, but renew it every two years. Just last month, as a matter of fact. To be clear and out of respect to those practicing the profession professionally: You wouldn't necessarily want me walking through your hospital door without what they call some "brushing up," but the option is open.

Anyways (that's twice now), I jabbered into that wireless microphone for just under an hour and managed to keep their attention (I cheat partway through by showing a video of my neighbor blowing up a silo with a homemade cannon… it's easier to "win the day" if you have your own cannon) and I don't know what they absorbed of use, but I hope they heard the part that came from my heart, the part about how life is richer if you run with more than one crowd, how some of us follow the path more than the plan, and above all I hope they heard something of gratitude in my words: Gratitude for my freedom, for all the help along the way, and for their young spirits, because tomorrow everything depends on them.

BAD COFFEE

I would rank my coffee snobbery on a sliding scale some-where between "Slightly Snooty" and "Just Happy To Have Some." Of course I believe a ceramic cupful brewed at just the right temperature with fresh-ground, fresh-roasted beans and pure water that has never touched plastic tastes better than some supermarket grind from a can, and to say other-wise is to pretend there's no difference between grades of motor oil, hand loads versus factory loads, or a drop forged wrench as opposed to cheapo cast. That said, sometimes all's you need is to crank down a bolt on the rototiller, and some-times all's you need is to get going in the morning, at which point any one of your tin-canned or truckstop-distributed brews provides sufficient combustion and comfort. You check my personal coffee-making supplies situation right this minute and you'll find a can of mass market grounds right alongside the artisanal beanery.

So. High-end grind or Regular Joe joe, I'm good to go. But on one principle I have long stood in unrepentant opposi-tion: *flavored* coffee.

I still remember the first time I came across it. Early 1990s.

A friend's wife worked at a coffee shop in the mall, back when a coffee shop in a mall was still unusual. We stopped in, and I—a straight-up yellow-plastic-scooper Folgers boy at the time—was entranced by the aroma of snickerdoodle coffee, caramel toffee coffee, chocolate raspberry coffee, pecan pie coffee, butter rum coffee, and on and on. I chose a couple, took them home, and brewed them up.

You know how sometimes you think there's one more step at the top of the stairs and you stick your hoof out and there's nothing there? And you nearly fall on your face because you were expecting something a little more sturdy? And although you shoulda seen it coming, you feel like you've been snookered?

That's how I feel about flavored coffee. Smells great, tastes...something short of that.

Preserve your outrage and evangelism: This is about me, not you. One of my prime mentors—a West Point graduate of character, rectitude and success—drinks flavored coffee constantly. Still I admire him. Go for it. But over time I have so grown to love the pure bean I find any syrupy fakery a personal affront. (The addition of sugar and creamers is another character issue altogether, and I will leave it alone; I can wage this battle on only so many fronts.)

Last week, her vision blurred by a red-hot deal, my wife inadvertently purchased two pounds of flavored beans. Jonesing, I ripped into them before checking the label, which read, "A rich and creamy blend of vanilla, caramel and coffee liqueur flavoring."

I married for better or worse, with the ratio running lopsided to the prior. We wound up with those beans because my wife is overworked and frugal, and two cups a day, I am drinking that coffee until it is gone. The blend could be worse (were "mint" or "cobbler" or anything ending in "delight" involved, I'd have to tap out) although one wonders what sort of coffee bean requires the addition of "coffee liquer flavoring." Marriage and coffee require compromise. What we have here is a situation not of taste but of budget, and early on these window-frost mornings, I am Just Happy To Have Some.

BAD SANDWICH

Today at lunch I ate a sandwich of uncertain provenance. We await the results.

I was alone in the house and on leftover patrol. The sandwich—half a sandwich, actually, a neatly knived bisection—was carefully sealed in a plastic container. I am ever on the lookout for labor-saving devices, and pre-made sandwiches definitely qualify, so I placed it on the plate alongside the final scoop of last Wednesday's microwaved chicken broccoli rice hotdish, a couple of sweet banana peppers for health, and—so as not to grow weak come the waning hours of the afternoon—three fat slices of summer sausage infused with cheese. You have to take your vitamins.

I lit into the sandwich as my second course, after the hotdish. At first bite the bread seemed a tad over-moist, but I figured this was simply the result of storage conditions. I took another bite. I can't say it was the best sandwich ever, but it didn't smell bad. I admit this is not the bar as it is set by your leading gourmands. After the third bite I did the ol' peel-back to see if I could identify the condiments but they had merged with the rest of the materials. At this point I noticed the meat was of an indeterminate shade. Grayish. And yet, again, nothing olfactorily off-putting, so I chomped on. Duty, you know. Duty crossed with post-Calvinist guilt and clean-plate syndrome. Grandpa licking his plate because of the Depression, the coal burned to power the refrigerator, all of it came into play. Possibly also a habit of regularly eating more than I need eat.

I had moved on to the peppers and summer sausage when my wife called on an unrelated topic. Say, I said, That sandwich in the fridge...what'd you put in that? Didn't make it, she said. Your daughter made it. For school lunch. Two days ago. It was on the counter last night when I got home. I put it in the fridge and was going to ask her about it tonight and review our school lunch leftovers disposal protocol.

Oh, I gulped.

I have been blessed over the years with a Kevlar stomach, but this is not the kind of thing you brag about lest you tempt fate and anger the god named Ralph. What I can tell you at this point in our one-sided exchange is that as I type I am three hours out and feeling fine but assuming nothing. Should I take ill there will be nobility in it, having been struck low while attempting to extend the family's winter provisions. Furthermore a few skipped meals will only magnify the effect.

But: Fine for now. Ears feel a little weird, but that could be just the fourth cup of coffee. Also, everybody in the house but me has a cold. I would like to think this speaks to my constitution, fortified as it is by certain self-indulgences, including a chair-nap after lunch no matter what—or perhaps because of what—you had for lunch.

I close with hope and this specific salutation: Eat no sandwich of unverified provenance. Which is to say not only *what*, but *when*.

NOTE: *Read the next column for a remarkable update on the sandwich situation.*

BUMPKIN TRAVELING / SANDWICH UPDATE

Due in New York on Tuesday, I scanned the weather reports and moved my flights up to Monday. The hitch in this plan? I made the call just three hours before the final Monday departure. This precipitated two separate hour-long on-hold sessions, unreasonable blood pressures, a new suitcase-packing record, angry sweating, and a series of life-choice reconsiderations on the part of my wife.

I drove to the airport like the accelerator was a cockroach, arriving just in time to learn the flight was delayed beyond my connection time in Chicago. I stayed cool and in five minutes (and with the help of a friendly agent) (these things should be noted even when they don't support the narrative theme) booked a later flight.

Then came a mechanical delay. And bad weather. And de-icing. And that moment when you're locked in the plane at the gate and your airline app announces you're clearing 30,000 feet—untrue, and time travel of a different sort. When I finally did debark in O'Hare I had five minutes to cover fifteen minutes of airport.

Long-gone are the days when you could sprint from the curb to catch a flight, but gate-to-gate sprinting thrives, and I've always felt sorry for the flush-faced losers humping along short of breath and long on panic, in this case me: Backpack bouncing, roller bag banging off my heels, every other person in the airport either headed in the opposite direction or wandering like they're looking for their contacts. I made it, arriving in a last-second tie with another hyperventilating laggard. We stumbled across the jetway finish line and into our seats.

At LaGuardia a police blockade delayed the rental car shuttle bus for over an hour. As the cars all around us honked nonstop, I didn't care. I'd made it to New York. I pulled off my backpack, leaned back, and relaxed. A less-seasoned traveler would have blown it. How lovely it felt, when the shuttle arrived, to stroll for the car rental counter knowing that back home the blizzard cancellations were already stacking up. Less lovely to realize I'd left my backpack on the bus. I whirled, and yanking my roller bag so hard it trailed me in the horizontal, ran after the bus, already leaving the lot. Yelling and banging on the rear window, I worked my way up to the front until the driver hit the brakes and let me back on board. Now as I strolled to the rental counter my eyes were wide and my knees were liquid and it occurred to me that despite all the frequent flyer miles some of us are so steeped in rural bumpkinry we never quite kick it loose of our boots.

UPDATE: In last week's column, I described my unwitting —despite an abundance of clues—ingestion of a meat sandwich that had spent two days on the kitchen counter. While addressing refrigeration policies with my teenager, I saw her overcome by a fit of some sort, followed by a collapse into uncontrollable laughter. Between gasps, she revealed that before being placed on the counter, the sandwich had been in her car for between 2 or 4 months. This explains its lack of zing, but does not explain why I am still alive, or how far gone a sandwich has to be before I will eat it, and we close with all praise for unheated garages in winter in Wisconsin.

FAMOUS AUTHOR

Once a long time ago in a story I may have told before, I was in a coffee shop on the California coast when out of the blue two women at the table next to mine began talking about my books.

Now then. I was on book tour at the time, with a reading scheduled in the adjacent city that evening, but over the course of the women's conversation it became clear they were completely unaware of their proximity to this pending live literary explosion and were simply discussing my oeuvre of their own volition, a coincidence a widely-unknown Midwestern midlister such as I ranks as frankly astounding.

This is not fake self-deprecation. The tour to that point had been a real humbler, a series of what might be called "intimate" events with an average single-digit attendance allowing me to learn the names of everyone involved and still ask after their families. So it goes, far from home. The numbers don't lie, and Chippewa County is so far from Sonoma.

So of course I could hardly keep my eyes straight when I overheard two strangers saying nice things about my typing. I had a copy of the book I was touring for in my backpack, and it took everything I had to keep from casually drawing it out and then "accidentally" dropping it, front-cover-up, beside them. Oh how their eyes would widen. "Is it...is it...*you?!?*" they would yodel as they fanned themselves and begged me to read a favorite passage. In fact, once they recovered their facilities they would plead with me to stay put while they rushed home for their well-worn copies so that I might sign the whole works. Naturally this stir would attract attention, a crowd would gather, word would spread, and shortly the barista would slip over to humbly inquire if I might consent to stand on a chair in the window and share the bounty of my work with as many art-thirsty folk as the fire marshal would allow. Invariably the local media would show, one viral thing would lead to another, my publisher would extend the tour across an infinite stretch of all the major cosmopolitan outlets of the nation, send a fruit basket, and replace my rental car with a flannel-lined Gulfstream.

I reached into my backpack. The book—my latest at that time, the one I was on tour for, with the title *Visiting Tom*—was at my fingertips. "I heard he has a new book out!" said one of the women, excitedly. "Yes, yes!" said the other. "It's called...ah...um..."

"Oh it's right at the tip of my tongue," said the first woman.

"*Uncle Tom's Cabin!*" exclaimed the other.

"Yes! Yes! That's it!"

I let my backpack fall back against my chair. By the time I finished my coffee the women were gone. There were six people at the reading that evening. I recognized no one, but we had a lovely time. On the way out of town I refueled the rental car and got dinner to go at the gas station. I was careful to keep my receipts.

MAILBOX

Yesterday I did something magical, specifically walked out to the end of our driveway, placed an envelope in the mailbox, raised the plastic flag, then turned back for the house, trusting that the letter was safely enroute to its recipient. Say what you will about government programs, the postal service is one of those entities we love to denigrate even as we take its remaining reliable wonders for granted. And any yapping I might commit is muted by the fact that I regularly observe our local mail carrier feeding her beef cows in subzero weather while I am on my way to town for possibly a cappucino. And I don't have to drive with one window down.

But I have not come to declaim the USPS. Rather, on the walk back, I found myself considering our mailbox. It is a standard-issue big box store plastic job, green with a red flag, and otherwise unremarkable. Correction: It does sport a modest constellation of bullet holes, so it is not utterly without character, although around these parts, this sort of ventilation is standard issue and so unavoidable you might as well do it yourself right after you get home from the store.

I feel we are witnessing the decline of the golden age of

the homemade mailbox. Oh they're still out there: Mailboxes mounted atop spot-welded barn cleaner links or a logging chain that coils upward like a cast iron cobra, or a stack of similarly tacked-together truck wheel rims. A second mailbox mounted out of reach high above the main mailbox and labeled "Air Mail" or "Bills." Mailboxes made from springs or cables designed to swing out of the way if the snowplow operator (or Burt coming home from the bar) wanders a little too near the shoulder. The mailbox over there on Highway 10 mounted to a stunning replica of a vintage airplane (lately I see that has been moved back off the road and is now strictly decorative...I assume this is a preemptive preservation move).

I reiterate the term "homemade" to distinguish between novelty mailboxes in the shape of largemouth bass or tractors or whatnot but available at retail. The mailbox I grew up with was quite literally a plumbing project, made by an actual plumber using galvanized steel pipe and designed to swivel should it collect the dread snowplow strike. When the township redid the road, we had to move it. It turned out to be anchored with two chunks of concrete the size of twin pigs. We had to use the tractor and a hydraulic loader to shift it.

And here, perhaps, is where my concern with our mailbox lies. Not that it is visually unremarkable, rather that it can be knocked flat in a trice. I aspire—as I do in many categories—to be more like my brother John, a jack-of-all-trades who, after his mailbox was vandalized, undertook a radical free-standing redesign involving a hundred pounds of iron and half a package of welding rods. Soon enough some knothead knocked it flat in the wee hours. After righting it, John was pleased to report it had survived undamaged. But he was *delighted* to report that the ditch was scattered with bumper bits, the remains of a quarter panel, and at least one turn signal.

DAD MUSIC

Last night I attended a live concert in the company of my two daughters, ages 18 and 10. We left directly after dinner, our treat to their mother being a night alone in the quiet. As we passed down that section of the driveway where the tree branches meet and mesh overhead to form a leafy arch in warmer months, I flashed back to a family portrait we had taken there when the elder daughter was still a knobby-kneed mini-giraffe and the younger was a chubby-cheeked drooler. Now the elder is six feet tall, there are pickup-truck boys inbound, and there are college acceptance letters on the desk. The feeling in my chest was as if all of the breaths taken between that portrait and the present were pulled from me at once.

Thankfully, this sensation was inwardly—rather than outwardly—directed and I did not therefore veer straight into a maple. Instead, I declared how grateful I was to be going to listen to music with my daughters, and I think they sensed the old man was waxing wistful because they answered sweetly in the affirmative.

Then they asked me to turn up the radio.

Deep into this digital age, it's remarkable how the kids still want to listen to the radio. Now then: they don't want to listen to the *same* radio as Dad (as He Who Pays the Insurance, I reserve three buttons on the pre-select: country oldies, sports talk, and the legendary local station WCFW) (WCFW, where "FM means Fine Music" which is to say quite a lot of Neil Diamond and where my favorite thing of all is, even if Neil is only halfway through "Love On The Rocks," when it's time to do the weather, them folks at WCFW lift the needle and do the weather, and maybe next time Neil will get to that third verse).

But my theory about kids and music is, if the trip is short, my taste in music is secondary to the window into the world of my youths provided me if I let them listen to what they want and explain it to me as needed. I secretly delight in saying, "Who is this?" and having them patiently bring the bald guy up to speed. I found the old "That ain't music!" argument tiresome when I was young and am not much interested in it now that I am old. Everything changes, grampaw. And when an iffy lyric leads to a ten-mile discussion about consequential life choices with your soon-to-launch child, well, then the music has done its job, whether it fit your groove or not.

And then above all, life lessons aside, there is the exultation of children singing. Joyfully hollering out lyrics I can neither recite nor follow, the van moving down the road toward the future, my chest filling with breath again, perhaps just a touch less than before as it competes for space with my happy swelling heart.

ABOUT THE AUTHOR

Michael Perry was raised on a small dairy farm, worked as a ranch hand in Wyoming, got a nursing degree, then wound up writing and performing for a living.

At the time of this printing, he lives with his wife and two daughters in rural Wisconsin.

If time and technology allow, please visit SneezingCow.com for dispatches, photographs, and video.

Printed in Great Britain
by Amazon

83311129R00150